LOOK CLOSER

"It's a new world, and we must all think differently and honestly assess our own self-awareness. *Look Closer* pushes in all the right areas to keep a leader growing. Grab ahold of Dan's blueprint to uncovering your blind spots and to stay relevant as a leader. If ever there was a time that leaders need to face the brutal facts, it is in these uncertain and complex times when even more is needed and expected from leaders. This book is a treasure chest of ideas to help you do just that."

Lisa Paley
President, HALEON North America (formerly GSK Consumer Healthcare)

"Dan's body of work and approach get at the heart of what drives an organization. It's people and their passions. His genuine and authentic approach to everything he works on demonstrates to anyone truly listening that the 'how' is as important as the 'what.' I learn something new that I can put into practice every time l speak with him."

Jason Reiser
President of MPG (former senior leader at Family Dollar & Dollar General)

"Wow! Once again, Dan has challenged us to look inside first and prioritize, develop, and enhance the most important 'capital' in our lives … human capital!"

Chris Dimos
Chief operating officer, AccentCare

D1474196

"Dan Mack has been a part of my professional life and my growth as a leader for over a decade. He brings unique insights to interpersonal relationships and business interactions while doing it in a concise and actionable way. Everyone who has participated in his leadership events come away raving about what they have learned. Dan is a rare find in that he is extremely genuine and authentic. I guarantee this book will make a positive difference in your life."

Bruce Kramer
Senior vice president, North America Consumer Division,
Wahl Clipper Corporation

"When it comes to 'looking closer,' no one is better than Dan. He always gets to the literal and figurative heart of the matter, the issue, the founder, and the brand. Dan listens intently, without judgment, leaning in with an earnestness born of his wonder for what's possible. Dan is magic, and his closer looks into business and life are going to dramatically expand your thinking, and your options."

Craig Dubitsky
Chief innovation strategist of Colgate-Palmolive;
founder of Hello Brands and cofounder of EOS

"*Look Closer* offers a practical guide, measured in real life experiences, of how to be a better person and leader. In the age of hypercompetition, geopolitical risk, pandemics, and more, the true sense of competitive advantage just might be the principles Dan outlines in this new book."

Wayne Bennett
Senior vice president, Retail of ECRM/RangeMe

"Working with Dan Mack as a coach has changed me. He has helped me become an emotionally healthy leader and create high-performing teams. His approach is insightful and provocative; his blueprint is actionable. This is not a journey for the faint of heart but one of real courage, self-reflection, vulnerability, and self-discovery."

Stacey Ramstedt
VP of Marketing, Specialty Hair Care at Church & Dwight

"*Look Closer* provides amazing insight on self-discovery and self-reflection. Dan's research and coaching experiences in identifying and providing solutions to personal, relational, and organizational 'blind spots' are thought provoking. A must read for staying true to yourself while enhancing personal development and professional relationships."

Bob Ford
Vice president, head of US Field Sales,
Health and Wellbeing Collective (Division of Unilever)

"Just when you think that you've got a leadership trait mastered, Dan has a way of adding a new perspective, peeling away the outer layer. You suddenly realize that you've only scratched the surface. His thoughtful and insightful style has been helping people to become more empathetic and effective leaders for years."

Gary Gatton
CEO, Traditional Medicinals

"Dan has been a pioneer in bringing EQ and human dynamics to the forefront of leading high-performing teams. His coaching and leadership forums continue to bring people together to discuss vulnerability, courage, curiosity, and empathy as tools in locking professional and personal growth."

Nick Rini
GM, vice president, North America, i-Health, Inc., a Division of DSM

"Some people inspire us and leave lasting impacts on our careers. Dan put me on a path to look deeply at what type of leader I was and who I hoped to become. He encouraged me to not only write my leadership story but to convey it with transparency. Dan is a master at uncovering and sharing what makes successful leaders stand out, acting as a powerful and inspiring force in the industry."

Beth Stiller
CEO, Massage Envy

LOOK CLOSER

IDEAS ON
REEXAMINING AND
ELIMINATING PERSONAL,
RELATIONAL, AND
ORGANIZATIONAL

BLIND SPOTS

DAN MACK

NOAH MACK — EDITOR-IN-CHIEF

Copyright © 2022 by Dan Mack.

All rights reserved. No part of this book may be used or reproduced in any manner whatsoever without prior written consent of the author, except as provided by the United States of America copyright law.

Published by Advantage, Charleston, South Carolina.
Member of Advantage Media Group.

ADVANTAGE is a registered trademark, and the Advantage colophon is a trademark of Advantage Media Group, Inc.

Printed in the United States of America.

10 9 8 7 6 5 4 3 2 1

ISBN: 978-1-64225-536-2 (Paperback)
ISBN: 978-1-64225-535-5 (eBook)

LCCN: 2022915022

Cover design by Mary Hamilton.
Layout design by Wesley Strickland.
Illustrations by Brian Quiroga.

This publication is designed to provide accurate and authoritative information in regard to the subject matter covered. It is sold with the understanding that the publisher is not engaged in rendering legal, accounting, or other professional services. If legal advice or other expert assistance is required, the services of a competent professional person should be sought.

Advantage Media Group is a publisher of business, self-improvement, and professional development books and online learning. We help entrepreneurs, business leaders, and professionals share their Stories, Passion, and Knowledge to help others Learn & Grow. Do you have a manuscript or book idea that you would like us to consider for publishing? Please visit **advantagefamily.com**.

Dedicated to:

Pauline Mack for encouraging me to push through fear.

Thanks to:

Eileen Toth, Evan Mack, and the members of the Elevation Forum Leadership Group for creating a space to test out ideas and learn from an amazing, diverse community.

Special thanks to:

Noah Mack for your tireless editing, thoughtfulness, and creativity. You were essential to bringing this project to completion.

Lastly to:

Michele for years of love, grace, and modeling for me an open mind.

CONTENTS

FOREWORD

"It ain't what you don't know that gets you into trouble ...
it's what you know for sure that just ain't so."

Attributed to **MARK TWAIN**

I have spent most of my career, like Dan Mack, working with many of the world's smartest companies—trying to help them see the world more clearly and accurately and to build more effective strategies resulting from that clarity. Usually, the biggest barrier to this is not a lack of knowledge. Most large organizations have access to better information than I typically have and have teams of people dedicated to understanding a changing world. The problem to overcome is not a fact gap, but a perspective one. Companies are simply blind to opportunities and risks because of their preconceived notions, habits, and biases toward the known world. These blind spots have caused many companies to be slow to capitalize on emerging consumer trends, growing channels of distribution, and the digital transformation of commerce and media.

Finding blind spots isn't just a strategic corporate imperative but also a personal one. I'm writing this in the spring of 2022, during twenty-four months of massive disruption. Readjusting to life after this upheaval creates a unique opportunity for all of us to reassess how we go about our business and our work lives, and what you will read in the book that follows is an excellent foundation for that reassessment. We all need to develop new ways of connecting to each other in a world where we may see our colleagues less frequently in-person and be increasingly working in virtual teams and workspaces. Raising our interpersonal competencies will also require seeing the blind spots in how we are perceived by others, and how we perceive the people around us.

There are so many pieces of this book that you will read and say, "Of course ... why don't I do that more often?" The answer will be simple—unconscious habit. To borrow the language of Kahneman and behavioral economics, it's not just our thinking that defaults to "System 1" type thinking of unconscious pattern recognition and overrelying on assumptions and history, but our behaviors and our attitudes toward others as well. There is simply no better time to fuel your world with new perspectives, new habits, and new approaches. I assure you that the next couple of hundred pages will reveal that in Dan Mack's distinctive style.

Many of you reading this book may never get a chance to meet Dan or work with him personally, as I have been privileged to do for the last fifteen years. The specific learning points in the book that follow are essential but what I hope also becomes apparent is Dan's approach. Simplicity as opposed to overcomplicating topics, delivered in an incredibly efficient communication style, will allow you to easily digest each point along the way. You will also note that so many of the conclusions in this book are questions—promoting perpetual curiosity and interrogation of ourselves, our actions, and motivations. I'm sure Dan would be thrilled if you as the reader remembered nothing specific from this book but simply replicated his approach to the world by listening first, being relentlessly curious, and deeply committing to the success of those around you.

What won't come through in the book completely, though, is the visceral experience of talking to Dan—as one of the world's truly active listeners, Dan almost forces you, by example, to follow the principles he espouses within the following chapters. Thoughtfulness and empathy are emphasized, and I can assure you they are genuine hallmarks of the author—not just pieces of advice.

After finishing this book, you will be ready to be a better strategist, a better employee, and a better leader. I can also assure you that the best benefit of following many of these steps is a richer professional life—with closer connections to colleagues and a workplace characterized with more interpersonal understanding. And many a blind spot made visible.

Enjoy the read!

BRYAN GILDENBERG

Senior vice president Commerce, Omnicom Commerce Group, and former chief knowledge officer, Kantar Retail Consulting Practice

THIS BOOK IS DIVIDED INTO THREE SECTIONS:

PART 1. PERSONAL BLIND SPOTS. A summary of the individual biases, misbeliefs, or misconceptions hindering personal effectiveness and insights into how to expand your self-awareness, mindset, and results.

PART 2. RELATIONAL BLIND SPOTS. An outline of the one-on-one communication dynamics that often disrupt healthy relationships and ideas on how to improve your personal impact with others.

PART 3. ORGANIZATIONAL BLIND SPOTS. An assessment and interpretation of the blind spots hindering group cohesion, and strategies on how to improve team health and holistic momentum.

THE BLIND SPOTS

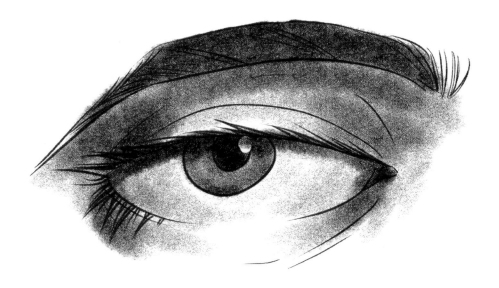

INTRODUCTION

WE ALL HAVE BLIND SPOTS

A therapist friend reminded me that "it takes transparency, courage, and emotional health to be open to the insecurity of self-discovery rather than choose to take the easy road and operate in self-deceit the rest of our lives." It's only natural to become fearful of how others perceive our weaknesses, when the alternative, courageous self-discovery, can be threatening, yet so rewarding. Every instinct is telling us as humans that we should run from pain. Our fight, flight, or freeze instinct kicks in and frequently takes the form of denying (fight), ignoring (flight), or doing nothing (freeze).

The adage "We don't see things the way they are; we see things as we are" is the guiding narrative of this book. We all suffer from hidden personal, relational, and organizational blind spots because our eyes look outward, not inward. My work as a coach, trainer, and consultant has forced me to look in the mirror at how I show up and how others see me. But make no mistake: I'm also on this endless journey. I implore you to dissent, disagree, and maybe even discard certain ideas in this book. I, like you, have glaring blind spots in my life. This book isn't meant to provide the answers to all problems.

Instead, it's meant to prompt you in the right direction and provide a blueprint on how to spotlight blind spots quickly and effectively in your own life.

We all suffer from blind spots, personally, relationally, and within every organization we play in. They are hidden from your view, occasionally creep up on you, yet are easily observed by your friends, colleagues, and family, preventing you from achieving your full potential. Though this book is centered on how to excel in your professional life, blind spots bleed into relationships with friends, family, and your emotional health. Though the prospect of personal change is daunting to everyone, take comfort in the knowledge that these pieces of advice are entirely manageable. To quote the author and behavioral scientist Dr. Steve Maraboli, "Incredible change happens in your life when you decide to take control of what you do have power over instead of craving control over what you don't."[1]

Whether you're in a position of leadership or not, we're all managers of our own lives, relationships, and state of mind. Too often, we fall into the same problematic pitfalls. We lack courage in difficult times when courage is needed, and we deceive ourselves into believing goals are unattainable or impossible. The most common and sneaky blind spot, however, is the tendency to take yourself out of the game before it even starts by playing too safe.

As a strategist and performance coach, I have studied personal, relational, and organizational blind spots for over thirty years. In my practice, I facilitate leadership events with diverse groups of sales and marketing associates, and I am always on the lookout for clues on why some teams are successful and others are not. This book is a curation of over ten years of facilitating discussions with some of the best companies and leaders in the world. The ideas shared in this book have been debated and discussed within my forum discussions by leaders from Walmart, Target, Walgreens, CVS Health, P&G, Unilever, Amazon, Google, Twitter, and many of the best challenger companies in the health, wellness, beauty, and consumable space. I've also been a follower, a leader, and a teammate, but most importantly, I have been a student of this topic for years.

Blind spots are subtle, sneaky, and as the name suggests, hidden from us. The leader who asserts their authority by texting during a newcomer's presentation, the woman who refuses to share control with peers during team meetings, the smooth-talking salesperson who unknowingly comes across as a con. Blind spots are our shadows, and when left unchecked, they can be detrimental to all aspects of our lives: from relationships with a significant other to reputation and productivity within the workplace. We're all certain we've cracked our own code, but it takes courage to admit vital parts of the code are hidden behind impenetrable firewalls. Constructive feedback, vigilant self-examination, and openness to dissenting points of view provide the necessary light to overcome our shadows.

Whether you are a leader, working for a large organization, or are an independent consultant, the healthiest and most impactful people are not afraid of the truth; in fact, they pursue it. As you move through this book, hold your views with an open hand. Don't clutch to your beliefs. Be willing to question whether the foundational strengths in your life are a double-edged sword that consistently causes self-injury.

This kind of book will naturally attract high performers who secretly strive for perfection, which is why I want to put your mind at ease and emphasize that perfection isn't the goal here. Brené Brown, author of *The Gifts of Imperfection,* wisely tells us, "Perfectionism is a self-destructive and addictive belief system that fuels this primary thought: If I look perfect, and do everything perfectly, I can avoid or minimize the painful feelings of shame, judgment, and blame."[2] For some, this journey of self-analysis will begin right now, and for others, it's been a defining part of their life. Accepting imperfection as an inevitability is the first step to objective personal examination.

Accepting imperfection as an inevitability is the first step to objective personal examination.

This book is divided into three distinct sections: personal, relational, and organizational blind spots. Take a moment to ponder the following questions and reflect on the implications for your own life. Each question will be answered in various chapters throughout the book, and it's important to gauge where you currently stand to calibrate where you wish to be.

- How do I affect others, and what must I learn, relearn, or unlearn to be effective?

- What blind spots negatively affect my relationships, self-awareness, and personal impact?

- Am I as relevant to my company, customers, and friends as I think?

- Am I present, transparent, and vulnerable, embracing the moment with others?

- Am I effective at sharing my personal story and embracing others' stories?

- What are the mindsets, behaviors, and strategies of high-performing teams and organizations?

- What is the psychology and mindset of top performers in all facets of life?

- What are the lies, biases, or roadblocks that can hinder my own personal plan?

This book is the culmination of ten years of personal research and insights gathered within the Elevation Forum Leadership gatherings, and it should not be quickly consumed. It is meant to be read chapter by chapter, but if you prefer to jump around, I invite you to do just that. Go through these ideas slowly and meticulously, ponder the ideas; there's a lot packed within each page.

PERSONAL

When I was in elementary school, high school, and college, and even during the beginning of my professional life, I would suffer from public speaking panic attacks. It was brutal, embarrassing, and a burden I carried for many years. It was a monkey on my back that hindered every part of my life. I had started to believe a lie that public speaking stress and social anxiety had become my story. This was the beginning of my journey researching, studying, and wrestling with improving my own personal impact. This section of the book is packed with ideas, research, and insights you can personally practice in your own life.

We all have more bad days than we would ever admit to. Our humanity and an occasional lack of discipline often get the best of us. When the pressure turns up, we get sloppy, and we often lose our way. I've studied human performance for three decades, and I am still a novice in managing my own mindset. Some days I am victorious, and other days I fail miserably. Our own lives can be humbling, which is why we must expand self-awareness. *Talent Smart* has tested the emotional intelligence (EQ) of more than a million people and found that 90 percent of high achievers have high EQ.[3] They possess the ability to manage their own emotions well and stay in healthy relationships with others. *Their internal process centers them and helps them make peace with fear.*

Creativity and originality are high-risk, high-reward traits. Coming up with an original idea or approach goes hand in hand with self-doubt for a reason—it's uncharted territory. To think outside the norm, it's essential to acknowledge how comfortable the norms can be. We often shy from discomfort and retreat from pressure because we are out of our comfort zones. Being at peace with the forces of volatility, uncertainty, and ambiguity are the prerequisites to creativity and originality. It's rooted in *mindset.*

If the inability to be an original and the tendency to succumb to negative outside pressure is one end of the performance spectrum, then the opposite end is overconfidence. Those who are driven by ego frequently miss critical input from peers. They're unable to admit when they're wrong, which makes it incredibly difficult for others to break through the thick wall of certainty surrounding them. Additionally, people suffering from these forms of blind spots often lack the ability to unlearn behaviors that served them in the past but now impair their potential.

Only you can remedy the weaknesses in your own life, and this section is meant to encourage self-examination and an honest critique. It is also a summary of practices and insights to help you show up better.

What's your process for personal impact?

"Blind spots are often rooted in certainty. We have all been given rules, scripts, and ways of thinking that simplify our lives. And some of them are even right."

THE IMPOSTER:
TAKE OFF YOUR MASK

"If I am estranged from myself, I am
 likewise a stranger to others."

BRENNAN MANNING

A few years ago, I was moderating a training conference with the senior leadership of a small, emerging company. During the meeting, I asked the CEO to share a moment that had transformed how he now leads. This individual was truly loved, admired, and respected by the members of his team because he was known for inspiring others with both his head and his heart. His response to the question shifted the atmosphere immediately, bringing tears to some people's eyes.

After a successful prior ten years at a company, he had lost the support of his team and had grown apart from his boss. He recalled walking the city streets until 4:00 a.m., feeling bewildered and empty as he assessed leaving the company because he felt he no longer fit the culture. As he shared the story, recounting the feelings and stress it put on his family, tears filled his eyes. He paused and shared, "That emotion is still with me." It was a moment of truth and openness. Everyone recognized the authenticity of this special leader because he had removed his mask.

Many of us have had these moments and empirically understand this feeling. It has been estimated that 70 percent of people suffer from the "Imposter Syndrome" at some point in their lives, that internal belief that one day we will be discovered as a "fraud."[4] When we don't feel genuinely confident, we fall into bad behaviors. These fraudulent feelings occur at all levels and can happen to anyone, but the most confident leaders are humble and have made peace with the imposter.

The late Franciscan thinker Brennan Manning said that if you are serious about leadership authenticity, you must take off your mask. "While the impostor draws his identity from past achievements and the adulation of others, the true self claims identity in its belovedness."[5] Leaders who are defined by personal accolades typically miss the mark. The leaders who are truly transformational are relational, are transparent, and connect on a deeper level. Manning continues, "In a futile attempt to erase our past, we deprive the community of our healing gift. If we conceal our wounds out of fear and shame, our inner darkness can neither be illuminated nor become a light for others."[6]

Are you courageous enough to truly share from the heart? Are you vulnerable and strong enough to take off the mask and genuinely connect with your team?

None of us likes perfect people. In fact, those who feel flawless typically are not great leaders. As the adage goes, "Never trust someone without a limp." *We want to experience others' humanity and understand their story.* Said another way, "perfection in imperfection" is what influences others. Are you comfortable being known?

Are you courageous enough to truly share from the heart?

My leadership and coaching philosophy was birthed in a home that struggled with my father's substance abuse. That was coupled with a slight stutter growing up and occasional social anxiety. This background makes me more sensitive to those trapped by their pasts and helps me empathize with others. I am not controlled by my story, but it always informs how I see the world.

I have noticed five behaviors that the healthiest leaders exhibit.

1. They are comfortable listening and do not need the spotlight.

2. Outside validation is unnecessary because their achievements internally fuel them.

3. They initiate courageous conversations and do not become defensive when others oppose them.

4. They are comfortable with ambiguity and are not threatened by opposing views.

5. They are curious about what they do not understand and are open to changing their minds.

Imposter syndrome is rooted in a belief that you are not enough, and as a result, you suffer from feelings of inadequacy, self-doubt, and insecurity. It creates an insatiable need for external affirmation and causes stress, anxiety, and fear.

Are you falling into bad habits, or is the imposter taking you away from bigger personal accomplishments? What's your process (or personal framework) for tapping into your very best on a consistent basis, and who is your trusted *consigliere?*

WHAT NOW?

When does your imposter show up? What does it cost you, and what one thing can you practice today to embrace your true self?

"Without exposure to potential failure, there is no risk."

BRENNAN MANNING

HOW PERCEPTIVE
ARE YOU REALLY?

"Emotional intelligence (EQ) accounts for
80 percent of career success."

DANIEL GOLEMAN

When I was a young manager, I designed a coaching workshop for a group of even younger associates. Two hours into the program, I felt like I had nailed it. Everyone's body language seemed expressive and open, and there weren't any participant questions as we ended the meeting. At the end of the training, three members of the team walked up to me and shared that a handful of the quieter attendees in the room felt confused and overwhelmed with the content I had shared. I was embarrassed, but a lesson was learned: most people don't always share what's on their mind, and we are not as perceptive as we may think. We always show up better in our heads.

Do you know without a shadow of a doubt that your relational communications are effective, and do you believe you have an accurate assessment of how you show up with others? Life, business, family, and friendships are a juggling act of varied emotions, and one's emotional intelligence (EQ), the ability to exercise empathy and make decisions prudently, is the ultimate cohesive.

When in a meeting, are you encountering colleagues who prematurely jump to conclusions, demonstrate defensiveness, and assume the worst in others? It is demoralizing to sit with know-it-alls who hijack discussions and struggle to receive constructive critiques from others.

People with high emotional intelligence rarely monopolize conversations, nor do they interrupt others in midsentence, inspiring openness and trust. They embrace collaboration and demand constructive feedback while protecting relationships. They are in control of their internal emotions, skilled at knowing "when" and "how" to speak to others.

Recent research by *The Economist Executive Education Navigator* showed that most executives have a very different perception of themselves than their employees. Ironically, these executives are constantly seeking self-improvement, but they are focusing on the wrong areas. Executives regularly cited that technology and finance are two themes they most wanted to improve, while employees ranked leadership, emotional intelligence, and other softer skills as the attributes that need special attention.[7] What is emotional intelligence, and are you emotionally literate?

Daniel Goleman's classic, *Emotional Intelligence: Why It Can Matter More Than IQ*, contends that EQ is as important as IQ for personal success. Goleman believes emotional intelligence is a human skill that can be taught, practiced, and expanded.[8]

Let's take a quick look at the four domains of EQ:

1. **SELF-AWARENESS:** Everyone must understand how they affect others to be successful. We all want to feel safe when speaking with a leader, but safety is hindered when a leader is disengaged, apathetic, disinterested, or angry. Individuals with strong self-awareness recognize their own emotions and

are cognizant of how they impact others. How do others experience you?

2. **SELF-MANAGEMENT:** Leaders must tame impulsive, dysfunctional behaviors and practice self-control. People who are unpredictable are perceived as chaotic, untrustworthy, or unsteady. If you come across as a loose cannon, others oftentimes become fearful of being honest with you. Individuals who self-manage their emotions are adept at working through stress and frustrations and are thoughtful in their communications with others. How do you manage your emotions under duress?

3. **SOCIAL AWARENESS:** Being conscientious of emotions and seeking to understand others' personal challenges is a foundational pillar of EQ. Empathy is not just innate; it's a muscle. It must be practiced and honed throughout your life. People with refined social awareness skills possess strong organizational aptitude and understand the importance of asking peers for their thoughts, considerations, and suggestions. Are you highly in tune with others' emotions?

4. **RELATIONSHIP MANAGEMENT:** In a high-performing, heavy-stress environment, it matters how well you listen, develop peer friendships, solve problems, build trusting bonds, and team up with others. Good "people skills" are the glue that holds teams and cultures together. Leaders who focus on relationships are inspiring coaches and are gifted at quickly resolving conflicts and building cooperative partnerships with peers and associates. How are you at building and protecting healthy relationships?

IQ only accounts for a fraction of a person's success yet is given paramount priority too often.[9] The softer social connections outlined above are the real indicators of a winner. Leaders who bring authentic inspiration create an atmosphere for growth and creativity. They motivate by providing a culture of openness, candor, and unity.

> **The more you pay attention to your own emotions, the more you increase your overall effectiveness and influence.**

Every time we fail to demonstrate self-control, we set ourselves up to be misjudged. All of us utilize mental shortcuts and judge behavior based on actions under pressure, but only those who practice their emotional intelligence can consistently overcome this reactionary thinking and fortify relationships in their life accordingly.

The more you pay attention to your own emotions, the more you increase your overall effectiveness and influence. Does your emotional intelligence fail you?

WHAT NOW?

When does your lack of self-awareness show up? What does it cost you, and what one thing can you practice today to expand your self-awareness?

"One can have no smaller or greater mastery than mastery of oneself."

LEONARDO DA VINCI

SUCCESS IS NOT YOUR FRIEND

"Everything that irritates us about others can
lead us to an understanding of ourselves."

CARL JUNG

A few years back, I was once sitting at a national sales meeting, and I noticed a group of younger associates buttering up the CEO over dinner. The senior leader could do no wrong, with every joke eliciting enormous laughter. He was at the top of the hierarchy and the center of attention. I thought to myself, any leader in this moment would believe they were Robin Williams's comic rival and the most interesting person in the room. My second thought was, "When have I been guilty of this behavior?" Everyone is vulnerable to warped perceptions when others fawn on them with praise. Why is it so difficult for leaders to see how they are truly perceived and how they affect others?

We start believing success in the past will lead to success in the future, but previous success is never our friend. Past victories can be invisible anchors holding us back, cementing mental models we are not even aware of. Executive coach Marshall Goldsmith frames it perfectly: "Most people think, I behave this way. I am successful.

Therefore, I must be successful because I behave this way."[10] We start to believe we are successful *because* of our dysfunctional behaviors, instead of *despite* these flaws, a logical fallacy we can all relate to.

> **We are all vulnerable to the allure of success, title, and achievement; the trick is to temper this desire.**

Organizational psychologist and researcher Tasha Eurich uncovered that 95 percent of people believe they are self-aware, but only 10-15 percent of people are "extremely" *self-aware*.[11] Most people struggle with internal feelings of insecurity or concern over their negative impact on others. The higher you climb, the more this delusion kicks in. We are all vulnerable to the allure of success, title, and achievement; the trick is to temper this desire enough to remain hungry. This starts with grounding yourself in the belief that you are not always seeing yourself accurately, and others are not free to share unfiltered feedback.

We all need truth-tellers in our lives. When you experience higher levels of success, you tend to shut out others' negative assessments of your efforts. You can easily become overconfident and too relaxed and lose a bit of your critical thinking. So, what is the answer?

PRIME THE PUMP. Since most people shy away from sharing difficult feedback, we must learn to naturally coax out the unfiltered truth from people who know us well and have insight into our blind spots or leadership vulnerabilities. By priming the pump and sharing your weaknesses up front, you give others permission to chime in and share additional thoughts on how they can help support your personal awareness.

DO THE WORK. The healthiest leaders I collaborate with are very comfortable showing the cracks in their personal armor. In fact, they relish these moments, understanding this is how you build authentic relationships and self-awareness. Are you courageous enough to work with a coach for an extended period? A trusted coach reminds you of behaviors you may already know but are not exercising, helping you to see yourself with clarity.

SELF-CRITIQUE. Failure is inherently uncomfortable, but we must be willing to examine a situation accurately while also sharing the learnings with associates. It takes courage to lay it all on the line and honestly examine what went wrong. We must all ask the difficult questions required for ongoing growth: Did we assign the right people to the project? Were we fully prepared, resourced, and committed to the initiative? Did we underestimate competition?

Self-critiques must be immediate, direct, and practiced openly within the culture. Are you brave enough to openly admit failures?

If you want to make personal gains, you must work closely with outsiders to help embrace your leadership reality, and deliberately practice having courageous conversations with peers, associates, or supervisors.

Confronting the truth of how you are affecting others requires fearless self-examination.

WHAT NOW?

When does overconfidence show up? What does it cost you, and what one thing can you practice today to minimize your overconfidence?

"You can't get away from yourself by
moving from one place to another."
ERNEST HEMINGWAY

THREE SINS OF LEADERSHIP

"One is often unconsciously surrounded
by one's own personal reality."

PAWAN MISHRA

Ten years ago, I coached a founder of a company who was brilliant, charismatic, and aspirational. He was also wildly dysfunctional, intimidated his employees, and was immune to constructive criticism. After receiving difficult yet practical feedback on a 360-interview survey, he proceeded to walk around his corporate office trying to persuade each person in the company on why their critique was not an accurate representation of his behavior. The moment was just another example of what all his associates were trying to convey in the interview. He had lost complete perspective and was not coachable. Are you ever accused of shooting the messenger, or minimizing personal feedback with peers, family, or people you trust?

The more power one possesses, the more deceived one can become. Title, influence, and status can leave you in a bubble. We become out of touch, and our own insecurities take over, amplifying our vulnerability to manipulation, defensiveness, and bad decisions. Power can be poisonous, and we are all susceptible to its venom.

Many of today's most interesting organizations are digitally native and boundaryless, leaving their traditional competitors in a state of panic. The new economy has left many organizations unprepared and without answers after disregarding their customers' changing needs for years. If you are not an emotionally healthy leader, you are vulnerable to a fall.

WHAT GETS IN THE WAY?

Over half of senior leaders fail within their first eighteen months of taking on a new role.[12] My research suggests that, for most, a lack of leadership health is a prime factor. Everybody is insecure on some level. Chances are that your least attractive attributes are seen by all, and hiding these insecurities hurts you much more than you think. No one likes a perfect person, and leadership insecurities operate similarly, hindering our ability to honestly listen to feedback and lead change. When we feel insecure, we often pick one of five coping mechanisms: denial, repression, projection, rationalization, or outbursts of emotion.

> **Over half of senior leaders fail within their first eighteen months of taking on a new role.**

WHICH COPING BEHAVIOR IS YOUR RUNNING MATE?

When our fears get the best of us, we automatically shut down our critical thinking. Triggers become insecurities, and insecurities become blind spots, shielding us from honest feedback. If you are not hearing dissenting voices, you are more than likely operating in a bubble and don't even realize it.

Author Patrick Lencioni reminds us in his book *The Five Dysfunctions of a Team*, "Teams succeed because they are exceedingly human. By acknowledging the imperfections of their humanity, members of functional teams overcome the natural tendencies that make teamwork so elusive."[13] When leaders do not take their emotional health seriously the following dysfunctions set in:

LACK OF VULNERABILITY – failure to model vulnerability sparks defensiveness and a culture that covers up mistakes. Why is it that most leaders that hate being controlled are some of the most controlling? The most convincing people I know understand that vulnerability is an offering, and you must offer something up if you want to get the best out of people in return.

FEAR OF OPPOSITION – failure to embrace opposing views breeds a culture of groupthink. Any time a team embraces niceness over honesty, the culture falls victim to false unity. Can people within your team truly speak freely? Conflict and critique are essential for spurring creativity and rooting out problems within the organization before they fester. They are the lifeblood of innovation.

NO PRIORITIES – failure to articulate crystal-clear "limited" priorities will unknowingly lay the foundation for a lack of accountability. The highest-performing leaders focus on critical yet limited priorities (ideally three to five) and embrace robust, ongoing, candid discussions.

Any organization that does not address the dysfunctional behavior of its leaders is destined to fall. Emotionally flawed executives negatively impact the culture and the financial results of their respective organizations. Unchecked leadership insecurities create distrust and drain the energy and passion from teams.

Insecurities are part of being human. Embrace yours. Are you surrounding yourself with people who check your insecurities honestly and allow you to drop your guard?

WHAT NOW?

When do your insecurities show up? What do they cost you, and what one thing can you practice today to neutralize your insecurities?

"Trust is the essence of leadership."

COLIN POWELL

UNBRIDLED CURIOSITY

"Where the spirit does not work with
the hand, there is no art."

LEONARDO DA VINCI

My wife, Michele, is an artist, writer, and extremely creative person. She is one of those rare people that possesses broad political, historical, and international understanding, but you would never know it, because of her humility and desire to listen to others. Michele is practiced at staying open minded, allowing her to see patterns and relationships that others miss. She does not snap to quick judgments, nor is she enamored of authority. Where much of the culture has cemented and reinforced their outlook on even the most uninformed opinions, Michele takes the opportunity to pause and dig deeper. Her broadmindedness fuels her creativity and is potently contagious. Do others see you as curious, or are you too locked into your own views?

Walter Isaacson's research on the lives of Leonardo da Vinci, Albert Einstein, and Steve Jobs shines a light on the transformational effect of curiosity. They taught us that questions unlock the future. Tangible skills have an expiration date, while creativity and critical thinking are timeless. The dreamers connect dots and ponder new thinking. Unbridled curiosity is the lesson of da Vinci, Einstein, and Jobs.

Isaacson shares that da Vinci made no distinction between the beauty of art and science. Steve Jobs lived at the intersection of the arts and technology, believing this to be the intersection where creativity occurs, the magic of connecting dots. When Steve Jobs was dying, he was asked, "What was your best product?" His response wasn't the Mac or iPhone. He said, "No, making a Mac or an iPhone is hard, but making a team that will always turn out Macs and iPhones—that's the hard part."[14] Creatives ask different questions.

Walter Isaacson shared these thoughts during an interview with Wharton School's Adam Grant: "Leonardo da Vinci, I believe, is history's greatest creative genius. Again, that doesn't mean he was the smartest person. But he could think like an artist and a scientist, which gave him something more valuable: the ability to visualize theoretical concepts."[15]

Isaacson continues: "The most interesting geniuses are those who see patterns across nature's infinite beauties. Da Vinci's brilliance spanned multiple disciplines. He peeled the flesh off the faces of cadavers, delineated the muscles that move the lips and then painted the world's most memorable smile. He studied human skulls, made layered drawings of the bones and teeth, and conveyed the skeletal agony of St. Jerome in 'St. Jerome in the Wilderness.' He explored the mathematics of optics, showed how light rays strike the cornea and produced magical illusions of changing visual perspectives in 'The Last Supper.'"[16]

Da Vinci lived in a state of unquenchable curiosity.

Isaacson reminds us, "His [da Vinci's] ability to blur the line between reality and fantasy was a key to his creativity. Skill without imagination is barren. He had 7,200 pages of notes, providing so much info on one page and showing his mental leaps. They are the greatest record of curiosity ever created."

The curious ones question everything, even that which appears unquestionable. Author Warren Berger offers a three-step question sequence: **WHY? WHAT IF?** and **HOW?**[17]

Why?

"Why?" is a question that seeks to understand a problem. When you ask, "Why?" you are trying to uncover a need or shed light on a particular issue.

What if?

A "what if" question requires imagination and jump-starts the creative process. When you ask, "What if?" you are trying to uncover options: "What if we look at the problem through this perspective?"

How?

When you ask, "How?" you are looking for a practical solution: "How do we do it?" or "How will it affect others?" It is an "action plan" question and should attempt to execute on the plans uncovered by curious "what if" questions.

Da Vinci embodied this process yet would often take extended periods of time off to reflect. Isaacson reminds us, "Sometimes when you're creative, you accomplish the most when you seem to be working the least, because you're bringing things together, and you're letting them gel. You're intuiting what you're going to do." Pausing, pondering, observing, and questioning allow you to connect dots. Einstein, da Vinci, and Jobs understood that curiosity is the oxygen of all innovation.

WHAT NOW?

When does your lack of curiosity show up? What does it cost you, and what one thing can you practice today to embrace a more curious mindset?

"Prolonged thinking is the way to discovery."

JOE HERBERT

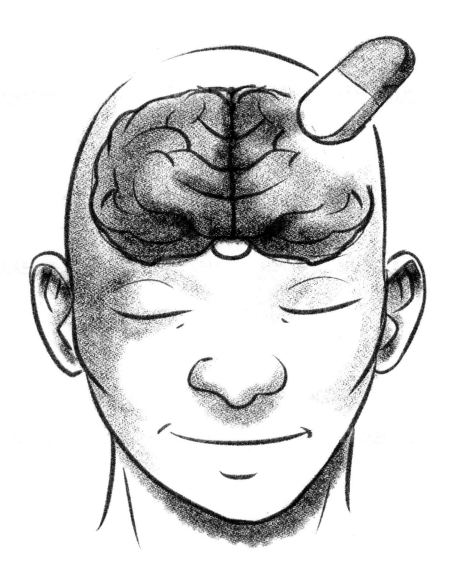

ARE YOU UNLEARNING?

"Perfecting oneself is as much unlearning as it is learning."

DIJKSTRA

My father, Don Mack, was introverted, humble, and a man of few words. He was drafted into World War II at the age of eighteen and as a father would rarely discuss what he experienced during those two years in Germany. I remember once asking him if it was scary parachuting out of a small plane at night. In a deadpan voice he reminded me, "I don't remember, since all I could see was the enemy shooting at my ass." A man of few words, with a dry sense of humor, he was someone who struggled with alcohol his whole life like so many young men coming back from the war. Drinking had become his running mate, something to take the edge off the experiences that had never been processed. Later in his life, when his health was failing, he finally got a little more control of his drinking. His health challenges had forced him to reconsider letting go of this old reassuring friend. Something had changed, and drinking was no longer filling the void. My dad had finally unlearned a debilitating behavior that had hindered him most of his life.

In his book, *The Structure of Scientific Revolution,* scientist Thomas Kuhn examines the phenomenon of the "paradigm shift." He describes it as the moment where enough errors in one's methodology or results force one to completely reconsider their lens. Kuhn believed a mental model would have to be replaced when the truth of one way of thinking became so weak that it was overhauled and replaced by another. He grew weary of his peers' discarding errors in their data rather than embracing the possibility that they were wrong.[18] Sound familiar?

We live in a world where the highest performers understand that unlearning old habits and overhauling their philosophies is a lifeline, not a hindrance or an admittance of guilt. They embrace the essential practice of unlearning detrimental habits that once served them because they understand that in those moments, an opportunity for growth presents itself.

> **The highest performers understand that unlearning old habits and overhauling their philosophies is a lifeline, not ... an admittance of guilt.**

Warren Buffett has long been a stalwart of consistency. However, labeling him as such belittles his uncanny ability to reconfigure his own lens and generate a paradigm shift. In a letter to Berkshire Hathaway Shareholders, he reminds us: "There's no magic to it … We haven't succeeded because we have some great, complicated systems or magic formulas we apply or anything of the sort. What we have is just simplicity itself."[19]

Buffett's philosophy is very straightforward: simplify everything and acknowledge that your frame of reference might be opaque. It is a brilliant mindset for those hoping to challenge their own habits. It keeps his team agile and ready to reassess their methodology whenever necessary. Buffett is the best at asking himself, "What's blocking me?"

Berkshire Hathaway's vice chairman, Charlie Munger, went further: "It is remarkable how much long-term advantage people like us have gotten by trying to be consistently not stupid, instead of trying to be very intelligent."[20] Word to the wise: quit trying to act so smart. Assuming you have all the answers ensures complacency and hinders feedback from peers.

What do you need to unlearn? And when is it time to unlearn old behavior? Most people wait too long and struggle to let go of old behaviors. It's natural, but it's deadly. We must become astute at pattern recognition and determining when an old model or pattern is obsolete.

In the *Harvard Business Review* article "Why the Problem with Learning Is Unlearning," author Mark Bonchek reminds us: "Unlearning is not about forgetting. It's about the ability to choose an alternative mental model or paradigm. When we learn, we add new skills or knowledge to what we already know."[21] One such mental model (or mindset shift) Bonchek offers is instead of "delivering a value proposition" to a client, be multidimensional in the relationship with them "fulfilling a shared purpose." That is a distinctly different mindset, and it forces one to reconsider the deeper (unstated) goals of a relationship.

Bonchek shares three steps to unlearning:

1. **RECOGNIZE THAT THE OLD MENTAL MODEL IS NO LONGER RELEVANT OR EFFECTIVE, EVEN IF THIS IS SCARY.**

2. **FIND OR CREATE A NEW MODEL THAT WILL BETTER ACHIEVE YOUR GOALS.**

3. **PRACTICE THE NEW MENTAL MODEL IN YOUR LIFE UNTIL IT BECOMES INGRAINED.**

If you believe all the same philosophies, strategies, and ideas you did twenty years ago, you may want to consider going back and reassessing those foundational instincts which are often overlooked. Knowledge expands, our lens widens, and occasionally we are wrong. After letting go of an old belief, it's then time to rebuild or reconstruct new perspectives that serve you better. Take the time to open yourself up to new frontiers of thinking, contrarian voices, and generally taking in new information. This can be the objective of your morning commute.

If you are struggling to change your mind, consider asking yourself this question: "Have you defined yourself by a belief, hindering your ability to let it go?" We all strive to be congruent, and it is often easier to rationalize an outdated belief than to kick it to the curb. Sometimes it is just too difficult to let a belief go because it is interwoven into the fabric of our lives and our social networks. Are you grasping onto outdated or obsolete beliefs or routines that you need to let go of?

WHAT NOW?

When do your limiting beliefs show up? What do they cost you, and what is one thing you can practice today to unlearn or let go of old behaviors that no longer serve you?

"When we unlearn, we step outside the
mental model to choose a different one."

MARK BONCHEK

WHAT'S YOUR PROCESS?

"Life shrinks or expands in proportion to one's courage."

ANAÏS NIN

Let me introduce you to Adam, an old high school classmate of mine from a little town in eastern Michigan where I grew up. Adam's family paid for his college tuition in full. He had money in his pocket, friends that loved him, and lots of time on his hands. Adam wasn't fond of attending college classes and spent most of his time hanging out in the dorms telling jokes to his mates, cutting class, and living for the moment. Adam was funny, creative, and very likeable. He was, and still is, an incredibly generous person who will give you the shirt off his back if you need it. I had not seen Adam for years and recently ran into him traveling back to my hometown for a family gathering. Life had not been kind to him. His lifelong lack of structure never allowed him the opportunity to build a career, a family, or much of a life. Sadly, his lack of discipline or process had cost him dearly. He was filled with regret, and I personally experienced his sense of loss as we reminisced over a drink. We all have an Adam in our lives, and it's heartbreaking to see personal disappointment and wasted talent. Does your process serve you?

Our biggest problem is not that our perceptions are wrong, but that they are right. Fear paralyzes us from acting on what we already know. This can blind us, and we become defensive as friends or associates share what they are seeing. Problems expand and intensify when we ignore, delay, or shun responsibilities. Monsters always get bigger when not confronted. It is far better to confront a fear early on than hope it will magically disappear. We spend so much of our time creating a map of the world that protects us from threats, enemies, and monsters. It is a much better strategy to deconstruct the map and confront fear.

Fear can be an amazing asset when channeled correctly. After all, fear is your chief defense mechanism and an essential aspect of what it means to be human. While it is important to listen closely to that internal instinct, never let it take the driver's seat in your process. Fear often masquerades as truth, distracting us from dreams, goals, and aspirations. It saps your energy and diminishes your courage by reminding you of insecurities and past failures. Fear fuels and animates Imposter's Syndrome, the internal worry of being exposed as a "fraud." Acknowledge and take charge of your fears before they hijack and derail your process.

> **Acknowledge and take charge of your fears before they hijack and derail your process.**

THE PROCESS

Insecurities, lack of control, and stress sidetrack most people. They can confiscate our defense mechanisms, motivating us to overwork while demanding perfection and feeding destructive behaviors. Many times, we inadvertently celebrate workaholism and emotionally lose our way. We forget that some things just need to be done adequately, while others need precision and excellence. It is so easy to forget that not everything needs to be perfect. Are you choosing your emotions, or do they choose you? A healthy mindset is the consistent outflow of one's daily practice and process. What is your process?

The healthiest leaders have constructed a blueprint that serves and guides them, keeping them on track and holistically fit. They choose their behaviors. Fear can seem enigmatic and daunting in the moment, but a reliable way to interrupt fear's grip is to pause and analyze the emotion through a preset checklist. The following is a model I utilize in my coaching practice:

1. **FEAR.** What is the biggest fear holding you back and why?

2. **REFRAME.** How has this fear served and protected you?

3. **LIES.** What pressures, triggers, or lies prompt this fear?

4. **ACCEPT.** When we fight things, we give them power. What imperfections must you embrace?

5. **PRACTICE.** What behaviors, people, and activities bring out your best?

Doctor Atul Gawande's classic book *The Checklist Manifesto: How to Get Things Right* shares a disciplined protocol (or checklist) to reduce medical infections by 66 percent. The research in medicine, like the arts, sports, and business, is clear: a disciplined process delivers results.

Gawande suggests creating a personal checklist between five and nine items, which you review each day to ensure you are staying on track.[22] Your process cannot be too difficult. Keep it simple.

A simple checklist is necessary to achieve success with consistent results. It protects us from failure and helps us remain in control of our own life.

What's your process?

WHAT NOW?

When does your fear show up? What does it cost you, and what one thing can you practice today to embrace your fears?

"The brave man is not he who does not feel afraid, but he who conquers that fear."

NELSON MANDELA

OVERCONFIDENCE CAN LEAD TO A FALL

"Overconfidence precedes carelessness."

TOBA BETA

I have always done my homework. Interestingly, everyone in our family always did their homework and still do to this day. Where was this habit formed, and why does it feel like it's always been a part of my life? My mother was from Canada, gained her master's degree in social work, and moved from Montreal to a small town in Michigan at a time when many women didn't lead independent professional lives. She was smart, courageous, a mother of five children. Pauline Mack was also a studier, and each night she would lay out her books, folders, and notes for the next day, thinking through her plan with thoughtful, detailed notes. My mom never allowed overconfidence to get the best of her. She taught me a valuable life lesson: don't let personal achievements distract you from preparing. Are there areas of your life where overconfidence could leave you vulnerable to a fall?

People who understate their personal skills are more effective leaders than those who overstate them.

According to recent research by leadership development group Zenger/Folkman, people who understate their personal skills are more effective leaders than those who overstate them. When we overstate our skills, act superior, or deny flaws, others lose confidence in us very quickly. We create a false image of perfection, which is both exhausting and sometimes hard to believe.

The most effective leaders don't overrate themselves or lie about their abilities; contrastingly, the research shows that they often underrate themselves. Peers respond well to *quiet* confidence. The quietly confident know what makes them effective, and their decisions reflect this efficacy without the need for salesmanship or fluff.

A study by Zenger/Folkman showed that the more we understate our accomplishments, the more others perceive us as leaders. Furthermore, managers who underestimate their personal skills create a more engaging and inspiring team atmosphere.[23] The research does not discourage confidence; it discourages *over*confidence. It reminds us that leaders who are too confident create auras that hinder their own personal development. The study emphasizes humility as a defining attribute of winning leaders.

Stay rooted in humility and develop your own personal awareness. Once a quarter, ask the strongest people in your network to honestly share how you positively and negatively affect others.

- Practice deep listening and allow others the freedom to interrogate your ideas.

- Uncover where your nonverbals may alienate or shut down others without knowing.

- Discover when you talk too much, interrupt others, and do not listen enough with the intent to truly understand.

All opinions matter. If you disagree with others, that's even more reason to take the time to discover how they are seeing you. You may not be as self-aware as you think.

Learn to love different, opposing, and dissenting voices, even if it stings a bit. Self-awareness will expand only when you allow yourself to stand in the line of fire. Nobody likes criticism, which is why most people are adept at suppressing it. When critical feedback is neutralized, the validity of the viewpoint does not disappear. Choosing to listen to that feedback and allowing yourself to be malleable in your thinking is how we check our overconfidence.

In 1930, the average S&P company lived for ninety years; now it is only seventeen years![24] Success can come quickly while failure can sneak up even faster. Advantages are almost always temporary.

What's really going on, and how do we thrive in a hypercompetitive world?

A chief executive of one of America's most successful companies asked Jim Collins, critically acclaimed business thinker: "How do I avoid falling, even when I am the best at what I do? And how would I know I'm falling if I were?" History shows that anyone, even the proverbial Goliath, is at risk of failing. We become overconfident, think we are entitled to our success, and lose track of the drivers that created that success in the first place. In some ways, Collins says that the best way to ensure success is to never believe you've found the recipe to it.

WHAT NOW?

When does your lack of humility show up? What does it cost you, and what one thing can you practice today to embrace humility?

"When the rhetoric of success replaces penetrating understanding and insight, decline will very likely follow."

JIM COLLINS

COULD YOU BE WRONG?

"I have not failed. I've just found 10,000
 ways that won't work."

THOMAS A. EDISON

During a coaching engagement a couple of years ago, I rehearsed with a client how to navigate a difficult upcoming customer meeting. We enjoyed a robust discussion on how he would maneuver the conflict and agreed on a constructive framework for managing his emotions under pressure. We spent ninety minutes outlining his approach, and he left energized and confident. Two weeks later he called me and shared that his meeting was a complete failure. I asked him if the ideas we discussed failed to deliver or whether an unknown challenge disrupted the engagement. He shared with me that anger got the best of him, damaging the customer relationship. His negative emotions ruled the day, and it took him months to recover. He had underestimated how heightened emotions could destabilize a long-standing relationship, and he misjudged the moment. When have you recently misjudged a personal relationship, and what did it cost you?

All of us are completely illogical creatures at times. We fail to see truths and allow predispositions and judgments to cloud our viewpoints. While it may be very difficult to reason someone out of their viewpoint, it is possible to refine your own reasoning by asking one question: *Could I be wrong?*

"Your conscious mind is basically an overconfident storyteller. You are on unconscious autopilot most of the day,"[25] says Tim Wilson, professor of psychology at the University of Virginia. And you are not seeing yourself accurately.

When we ask ourselves the simple question, "Could I be wrong?" we become vulnerable and open to truth without fear of retribution. This question creates a feeling of uncertainty that can often be uncomfortable and make us want to retreat to our own carefully curated set of beliefs. It forces us to leave that secure mental space and challenge foundational principles.

Jim Haudan, cofounder and CEO of Root, is one of the leading voices on engagement. In an *Inc.* article titled "How to Create an Environment That Fosters Truth Telling," Jim states: "We don't perform at our full potential; we perform at our belief level. And in the face of change, fear and anxiety often control our beliefs ... The antidote to this epidemic of ruthlessness is finding a way to safely have critical conversations, thereby creating an environment where people can be vulnerable, and explore the truths with which we are creatively dissatisfied."[26]

Our brains take the path of least resistance, looking for previous patterns or shortcuts and speeding up our decision-making process. This occurs on a subconscious level, making us vulnerable to being wrong. Let me remind you of these two notable examples:

- In 1962, the Beatles were flat out rejected by executives of Decca Records: "We don't like their music, and guitar is on the way out."[27]

- H. M. Warner of Warner Brothers back in 1927: "Who the hell wants to hear actors talk?"[28]

The benefit of hindsight gives us insight into how crazy these quotes are, yet the true value is in predicting these shifts while the cultural and financial current is flowing in a different direction. Are you able to enter scenarios with an open mind, and are you willing to challenge dearly held beliefs?

The scientific method is founded on the idea that a hypothesis must be critiqued by peers to test the integrity and strength of the finding. If a hypothesis cannot withstand the inquiry of others, it must be reassessed. That is the value of honestly assessing your views and the importance of third-party inspections. Skeptics are threatening to leadership but vital to the health of any organization.

Have you closed the door on new ideas, throwing up roadblocks in your thinking that impair your vision?

Are you able to enter scenarios with an open mind, and are you willing to challenge dearly held beliefs?

Whom do you trust to share the objective, unfiltered truth, while also helping you take ideas to the next level? Stay close to your most reliable and candid truth-tellers that are astute, honest, and invested in your success and emotional health.

The value of debate is to uncover the truth, not win an argument. A healthy debate will always help refine and catalyze one's thinking. If you want to avoid blind spots, listen to opposing views. Destructive argument is not an effective debate strategy, nor does it help you uncover truth. It is a defense mechanism, a knee-jerk reaction based in fear that will almost always keep you in the dark. Be constructive and seek to understand an opposing view. If you leave a discussion of dissenting perspectives with the same mentality with which you entered, then you probably missed something.

Next time you are confident about a big decision, ask yourself: "Could I be wrong?"

WHAT NOW?

When does your lack of openness show up? What does it cost you, and what one thing can you practice today to embrace more openness?

"Certainty is murderous."

PHILOSOPHER WILL DURANT

SELF-DECEPTION

"We gather information (selectively), interpret it (prejudicially), and recall it (unreliably)."

MARSHALL GOLDSMITH

Recently, I spoke with a friend that chose to step away from his leadership role within a family-owned health-and-wellness company after years of success. It seemed that the president of the company, who had recruited him from their former organization, was becoming unbearable due to his defensiveness and insecurities. I asked him if he had shared any of his thoughts with his boss, and he dejectedly responded, "No, and he wouldn't listen even if I did." After decades of coaching and counseling leaders, I am more convinced than ever that most leaders never hear the truth about how they impact others. Their view of themselves is a mirage, and their own self-analysis is distorted by lack of feedback and self-delusion. We all need candid coaches, advisors, and consiglieres who have the courage to shine a light on parts of our personality that often get the best of us. Garnering a group of trusted advisors who aren't afraid to speak their mind about your leadership style is vital if you want honest feedback on your quality.

In Marshall Goldsmith's book *Triggers,* he had thousands of leaders worldwide grade their performance. The results are shocking: 70 percent of leaders believe they are in the top 10 percent of their peer group. And almost every leader (98.5 percent) believes they are in the top 50 percent of their peer group.[29] This is a poignant example of how prone we all are to self-deception. Why do we all have such difficulty seeing ourselves accurately, and are you prone to this same problem?

Goldsmith's research clearly demonstrates that most people have an inaccurate perception of their personal performance. In a world where most leaders claim to embrace self-examination, how can so many be deceived? As Goldsmith says, "Our inner beliefs trigger failure before it happens. They sabotage lasting change by canceling its possibility." Mental models (or triggers) either neutralize us or set us free to create. They are installed in us and possess great power, whether we acknowledge them or not.

> **Most people have an inaccurate perception of their personal performance.**

TRIGGERS FUEL SELF-DECEPTION

High performers are oftentimes the most influential people in the room, suffering from a false sense of power and a belief that tricks them into thinking they can control the behaviors of others. They are mistaken.

If Goldsmith is right, our biggest struggle is implementing change, not just recognizing the need for it. Our triggers often catapult us back into limiting behavioral patterns. Frequently, they are not based in fact, but they are real nonetheless, dramatically influencing our subconscious, beliefs, and actions. When we are tired and let our guard down, we are even more responsive to triggers. Fatigue and energy depletion also create weaknesses in judgment and expose our vulnerabilities as leaders. For example, at the end of a long week of work, most of us hit a wall where we have a higher susceptibility and vulnerability to bad decisions and unconscious triggers.

Regardless of how our habits trigger our regression, Goldsmith shares one principle that is always effective in preventing it: "Any effort to contain our normal impulses in the face of other people's obstinacy can be high depletion. Creating structure is how we overcome depletion. When we have structure, we don't have to make as many choices; we just follow the plan."

Structure gives us freedom, and we become less reliant on emotionally draining self-discipline. Structure drives results. Think about asking these structured questions each week:

- What is hindering or stunting our team's growth and internal alignment?

- What competitive threats, new risks, or customer trends should we focus on?

- What truly creates value for the customer, and what is getting in the way of the team having fun?

We all tend to favor information that confirms our opinions, true or not. Do not always trust your gut; build some structure to interrupt toxic biases.

What trigger is getting the best of you?

WHAT NOW?

When do triggers show up? What do they cost you, and what's one thing you can practice today to see yourself more clearly?

"Whenever you find yourself on the side of the majority, it is time to reform (or pause and reflect)."

MARK TWAIN

THE BEGINNER'S MIND

"I have no special talents. I am only passionately curious."

ALBERT EINSTEIN

When I think back to my own childhood, the end of summer was always a bit nerve-racking because school was right around the corner. I was an avid team sport athlete and music lover, so nothing was more demoralizing than going back to school and taking tests. Today I love learning, but when I was younger, I struggled with a fixed mindset, both in the classroom and on the playing field. Under pressure, I would freeze, and I found it difficult to remain mentally open. The Buddhist Zen Master Shunryu Suzuki reminds us: "The mind of the beginner is empty, free of the habits of the expert, ready to accept doubt, and open to all of the possibilities."[30] The most inspiring people I know embrace the beginner's mind to foundationally rethink problems through a fresh lens.

Many leaders become prisoners of their own ideas. Our research has consistently uncovered this phenomenon with entrepreneurs, senior leaders, and even in smaller mom-and-pop companies. They become too narrowly obsessed and attached to their predetermined game plan, and it comes at a cost. When I coach clients, I often wonder what this defense mechanism is that often kicks in with high achievers, hindering their ability to honestly assess their communication and management skills. It's a misguided sense of certainty and a lack of receptiveness to others' ideas that negatively impacts their judgment, courage to take risks, and subsequently their ability to dream. Why is dreaming an essential leadership behavior?

Dreaming is a dangerous business, and it reminds me of the old proverb "It always seems impossible until it's done." It demands a commitment to pausing, reflecting, and listening to others, observing what is before us in a fresh light. We must possess a childlike beginner's mind to birth a dream. The beginner's mind is where we open up and break through the fears or doubts that hinder our ability to create. It is rooted in mindfulness, playfulness, and daily rituals that encourage learning and honest assessments.

Dreaming is a dangerous business.

BIRTHING DREAMS

Science suggests we are more likely to discover and engage with dreams in our most vulnerable moments: in the morning, at night, and when we are least prepared. "The mind is a great servant but a terrible master,"[31] says author David Allen, but that's because our dreams and our reality are constantly at war, and our attention is at stake.

Christian Nellemann, founder and CEO of XLN, offers an insight into dreaming in the article "Don't Bore Your Customers." New ideas often emerge when our defenses are down. Ideas don't announce themselves; they are unplanned and unexpected. Nellemann states that many people believe they are most creative at the end of the day when they are tired. "When we're exhausted, the part of our brain associated with inhibition—the blocking or filtering of non-essential information from our consciousness—is less effective. This gives more power to non-essential ideas, lateral thinking, and our subconscious."[32]

The subconscious mind makes just about every single decision in our life. Reinforced by every type of bias, our mind defaults to conservatism and safe options. Experts say: "Decisions are made on a subconscious level before our conscious minds are even aware the decision has been made. They're automated responses. Our conscious minds save energy by engaging in short cuts. The brain also works hard to reconcile what appears to be an inconsistency, and often this reconciliation leads us astray. Built-in expectations and assumptions are exploited."

A PwC survey of more than a thousand CEOs stated "curiosity" and "open-mindedness" are the most important traits to thrive in this new economy.[33] And a study at the University of California-Davis showed that curiosity enhances one's ability to learn and retain new information.[34] An inquisitive mind encourages creativity, challenges norms, and is a catalyst for idea generation. Curious cultures are positioned for success. Are you developing your childlike curiosity muscle?

Shunryu Suzuki (*Zen Mind, Beginner's Mind*) once said, "In the beginner's mind there are many possibilities, but in the expert's, there are few."[35] The expert's mind is, in some ways, a trap. Though armed with knowledge, it's also burdened by it, and those who are "experts" are slower and less curious because of it. The expert's mind closes doors while the beginner's mind looks for a new door to open.

The most curious people I know have a beginner's mind. They willingly adopt others' views, see things as they are, and are free to reexamine their own assumptions, including their own preconceived opinions. Is every person your teacher, or do you relish being the expert?

The most interesting and endearing people I have ever coached are teachable. They have uncovered the mystery of being both accomplished and open to other ideas and critiques. The beginner's mind embraces the curiosity of a child and the rigor of a student. It is a special place to play, and the benefits are unmistakable. You see it in musical artists that never create the same sound twice or elite coaches who win regardless of historical team success. They are self-aware, creative, agile, open to self-evaluation, and are guided by a healthy self-image.

Most of us listen to others but hear an echo of our own opinions. Curious people ask bigger questions; they are attentive, interested in learning, and not in fear of confronting the truth.

Do you embrace the beginner's mind?

WHAT NOW?

When does closing your mind show up? What does it cost you, and what one thing can you practice today to promote inquisitiveness?

"The goal of practice is always to keep our beginner's mind."

SHUNRYU SUZUKI"

ARE YOU PRESENT?

"The point of power is always in the present moment."

LOUISE HAY

In a professional coaching or training setting, I have been told that I am a very good listener. In other words, when my guard is up, and the lights are shining, I make the grade and stay highly engaged and present. But that is often not the story in my personal life with my wife and two sons. I fall victim to being distracted, self-consumed, and stressed, sometimes causing me to miss the mark badly. Paradoxically, I have found that the most compelling and engaging people are not the most verbose; they are the ones who are highly present with others. Staying present is the ultimate gift we give to others, yet we often fail dramatically.

People spend 46.9 percent of their waking hours distracted, states a Harvard University study published by psychologists Mathew A. Killingsworth and Daniel T. Gilbert.[36] The study summarized 250,000 data points, assessing people's thoughts and actions as they meander through life.

Sadly, most of us operate on autopilot. Studies show that 91 percent of adults have their phones within arm's reach every hour of every day.[37] We are literally training ourselves to be distracted, and we are losing the ability to remain present.

Being present means mastering focus and awareness.

If you have the guts to focus on this one idea for a week, then I guarantee you will see tremendous growth in every part of your life: personal, business, relationships, and earnings. It is one of the most difficult skills, and it's fueled by the art of listening.

Being present means mastering focus and awareness.

Do you truly understand the benefits of effective listening? Listening demonstrates respect; it is the soul of cocreation, the root of collaboration, the essence of leadership, and the basis for higher-level engagement. Listening drives execution and attracts, retains, and helps develop talent. Listening makes you distinct.

We all have tendencies (or triggers) that distract us from being present or tuned in to others. What are your triggers, and what robs you of the moment? Is it anxiety, pressure, worry, or some other culprit? Once you are clear on what's distracting you, there are three strategies you can use to return to the present moment:

PAUSE. Very simple, yet powerful, pausing for an extra second or two prior to answering a question or addressing someone in conversation allows you to gather your thoughts, pick up nonverbal communication, and create more intimate, meaningful discussions with others. Practice the pause to capture the moment.

SIMPLIFY. The fewer words used (or the more concise your communication), the more aware you become of others' needs and interests in a discussion. Consciousness must be activated by silence.

INTERMISSIONS. We all need adequate transition time after a long week, between appointments, after phone calls, and in our personal lives. People who build in interludes or respites throughout their day have the energy and focus to stay in the moment with others. Periodic downtime provides you with the poise and energy to actively listen, which is vital to staying present.

Are you in the moment with others, or do you mentally drift? The most impactful people are following along word for word.

WHAT NOW?

When does distraction show up? What does it cost you, and what one thing can you practice today to improve your focus?

"If you want to conquer the anxiety of life,
   live in the moment, live in the breath."

AMIT RAY

HAVE YOU LOST YOUR EDGE?

"What should you forget?"

MACK ELEVATION

A few years back, I partnered with a client who had previously enjoyed entrepreneurial success. She had made a lot of money selling her business and, after sitting on the sidelines for a few years, jumped back into the game with the dream of doing it all over again. After a few years of flirting with her new venture, she quietly exited to the sidelines. It was a jarring failure.

Successful founders often lose their edge. They don't take the time to assess emerging threats, hidden risks, or their customers' evolving tastes and preferences. They take shortcuts and fail to refresh and revalidate their own perspectives. The problem is that ego and elevated self-image get the best of them. When have you personally lost your edge, and did you foresee it coming?

Remaining curious, humble, and open to other ideas is an internal battle. Personal achievements often hinder people's ability to listen to others who oppose their strategy. It blinds them from taking counsel on innovation, strategy, or new approaches, stopping them from asking the important questions. Leaders who have enjoyed previous success often fail to ask the question, "What's different this time around?" Or perhaps the better question: "What should I forget?"

ARE YOU GUILTY?

I have experienced this in my own life. After helping launch the PURELL brand, I was asked to help reposition and lead sales at DenTek Oral Care, but I found myself flipping through the same pages of my old playbook. My playbook was out of date. What worked beautifully with the launch of a new experiential product like PURELL was not as important for a specialty oral care product. I should have changed my strategy quicker—but previous success blinded me.

Peter Drucker once stated, "Half the leaders I have met don't need to learn what to do. They need to learn what to stop."[38] We all possess a roadmap that we habitually reference when assessing new challenges. Often, our roadmap becomes outdated and doesn't account for higher levels of volatility, uncertainty, and hidden complexity surrounding us. Are you guilty of falling in love with the sound of your own philosophy, or are you open to asking different questions?

It's vital that personal playbooks do not get in the way of self-assessment, curiosity, and others' perspectives. When we embrace curiosity, we stop assuming we understand concealed motives or needs. We open ourselves up to critique.

In my leadership forums and coaching practice, we discuss the power of asking uncommon questions. I often observe leaders who veer away from asking difficult questions because they have not built a culture that welcomes honest feedback. These cultures are often emotionally unsafe, inconsistent, and not practiced in courageous discussions. Just like with buyer discussions or any high-performing team, leaders must be able to ask (and listen to) difficult questions. This allows you to modify your roadmap as you encounter changing information. Are you brave enough to ask these three difficult questions?

- Why do people really leave this organization, and how am I personally a part of the problem?

- Where have I failed to create a culture that honestly questions authority and strategy?

- Is my team having fun, and what fears are hindering organizational cohesiveness and impact?

WHAT HAVE YOU FORGOTTEN?

The questions we ask ourselves set the tone for how we enter conversations and how we work through conflict with others. The right question invites us to reassess old scripts and negative experiences that mask our view of the world. We all need to be courageous and ask, "What have I forgotten?" and even more importantly, "What should I forget?"

The people I admire thoughtfully question themselves.

WHAT NOW?

When does your stubbornness show up? What does it cost you, and what one thing can you practice today to reassess your status?

"We run this company on questions, not answers."

ERIC SCHMIDT

ARE YOU AN ORIGINAL?

"The reinvention of daily life means marching
off the edge of our maps."

BOB BLACK

I was the leader of sales for GOJO Industries and the inventor and marketer of PURELL Instant Hand Sanitizer during the launch of the brand into the North American marketplace. What an amazing journey that experience brought to my life. The product was unique for its time, almost magical. It was transformational for so many children with compromised immune systems and professionals in healthcare settings. Throughout the COVID pandemic, hand sanitizers became a vital part of our day, a fixture in every place of work. The PURELL experience taught me a valuable lesson: Always be distinct and work to become an original. Originals have staying power.

Strategist, professor, and author Rita Gunther McGrath reminds us that "competitive advantage is transient."[39] Our current advantages are not sustainable. Brand loyalty is at an all-time low, and no one is insulated from competition for long. All of us must learn to hold our business assumptions, philosophies, and advantages with an open hand. This way we birth new ideas and garner originality.

According to the Conference Board, "20% of public companies experience a growth stall—losing half of their market capitalization due to poor strategic decisions."[40] They start losing their consumers, their differentiation fades, and they become replaceable. According to Fred Reicheld of Bain Consulting, the average US company loses 50 percent of their customers every five years, a defection rate of 10–30 percent per year.[41]

Plain and simple, most companies will lose their advantage at some point.

Organizations hold on to their ideas too long. They lose their way, their identity, and often the trust of their teams. This is true of leaders as well. Where are you holding on too tightly? I want to share some ideas and warning signs on why organizations and leaders fail and the behaviors behind them.

> **Most companies will lose their advantage at some point.**

Dartmouth business professor Sydney Finkelstein wrote in his book *Why Smart Executives Fail: And What You Can Learn from Their Mistakes* why businesses fail due to certain behaviors:[42]

- A flawed executive mindset that distorts everyone's view of reality

- Breakdowns in communication and trust

- Insecure leadership hindering course correction

Essentially, falls are driven by arrogance and complacency, by not understanding new competitors and a culture that doesn't encourage internal dissent or creative tension. So how do you improve your awareness of threats and attacks? Three questions must be asked at every off-site meeting:

1. What do we not understand? (The known unknowns)

2. What do we think we understand—but we don't? (Our blind spots)

3. What are the things we do not know we don't know? (The unknown unknowns)

Finkelstein argues that the most adept leaders, the ones that transform their employees into stars, possess five attributes: fearlessness, competitiveness, curiosity, high integrity, and authenticity.

They also have an "outward focus" on the changing landscape and competition, allowing for freedom to create original ideas. In Wharton School professor's Adam Grant's book *Originals,* special leaders are characterized as independent "original" thinkers.[43] They are nonconforming because they practice brutal honesty, embrace risk, and nurture a culture that unleashes originality.

The common threads are courage and honesty, while allowing others to take a leadership role. Are you watching the wrong competitors or reassessing your business and your competitive assumptions? Are you strong enough to question your own behaviors, listening to all the voices on your team? Who helps you see yourself?

WHAT NOW?

When does your lack of understanding show up? What does it cost you, and what one thing can you practice today to critique your professional competitive position?

"It is good to see ourselves as others see us. Try as we may, we are never able to know ourselves fully as we are."

MAHATMA GANDHI

THE MYTH OF CREATIVITY

"The key question is not 'How can I push
harder?' but 'Where can I let go?'"

MERETE WEDELL-WEDELLSBORG

When PURELL was acquired by Pfizer Consumer in 2004, it possessed over 60 percent of the market share within the United States and Canada. By 2010, prior to being reacquired by GOJO Industries, PURELL's market share had fallen well below 20 percent. The much larger acquisition partners did not dedicate the time, attention, and emotional support that GOJO had previously brought to the brand. And their lack of attention almost destroyed the brand. GOJO has since rebuilt PURELL, and it once again is a category-defining brand.

PURELL did not appreciate that the fundaments of their consumer business were changing right before their eyes. Lower-priced value brands were popping up everywhere, stealing a larger portion of their sales and chipping away at their market dominance. While PURELL was lying back and not innovating at the same rate that initially helped them build a loyal community of followers, the competition was adapting. They had taken their loyalists for granted and for several years did not introduce formulation and dispensing innovations that had built their brand equity.

Legendary former Intel CEO Andy Grove once shared that inflection points are when the "fundamentals of a business are about to change."[44] They are normally unannounced, sneaking up on an organization when they feel they're sitting comfortably. Have you ever been ambushed by a competitor's act of creativity?

Rita Gunther McGrath, a strategic management scholar and professor of management at the Columbia Business School, believes, "Today the dynamics of competitive advantage have shifted once more. Companies are achieving advantage through access to assets rather than ownership of them."[45] We all must learn to connect dots, uncover new alliances, and become comfortable stating, "I don't know." Creativity doesn't just happen by chance. Humility, curiosity, and silence all aid in birthing innovation and minimizing competitive threats.

ARE YOU TOO HEADSTRONG?

Adam Grant reminds us that solution-only thinking creates "a culture of advocacy instead of one of inquiry,"[46] where each person comes into the situation locked into their own way of solving problems while lobbying hard for that solution. They don't consider other perspectives.

When you're trying to come up with a creative solution to a problem, you might be tempted to buckle down and focus until you solve it. But recent research shows that taking breaks at regular intervals leads to better outcomes.[47] We tend to come up with redundant ideas when we don't take regular breaks.

DO YOU EMBRACE SOLITUDE?

The act of daydreaming is an act of creativity. Too much pressure, excessive thinking, or a heavy workload depletes us all. The research shows that if you want to increase your creativity, you must value daydreaming, moments of reflection, and solitude.

Author and lecturer Susan Cain wrote in her bestseller *Quiet: The Power of Introverts in a World That Can't Stop Talking* that we live in a world biased toward extroversion.[48] But creativity often requires a unique blend of collaboration and solitude, meaning extroversion is never an absolute answer. The literature shows that the most creative people are adept at exchanging and advancing ideas with others, while also engaging in quiet time.

The mystics got it right; you must be willing to wander in the desert to birth new discoveries.

> **If you want to increase your creativity, you must value daydreaming, moments of reflection, and solitude.**

DO YOU EMBRACE STRUCTURE?

David Allen, author of *Getting Things Done* and *Making It All Work,* states that creativity does not require discipline if we have allowed the time for it.[49] Creativity comes naturally when we have cleared the way for it by having a trusted system in place for our projects, calendars, and commitments. We've made room to tap into our creative intelligence in an organic way.

Most of the creative people I work with design a plan for creativity. It doesn't just happen; an atmosphere for inventiveness is required. They spend a lot of time pondering, reading outside of their field of study, connecting dots, and talking with those who challenge their views. They are creative because they value it.

It is a myth that creativity is for the select few. We all have the potential to uncover new discoveries in the strangest places and at the most unpredictable times.

WHAT NOW?

When does your anxiety show up? What does it cost you, and what one thing can you practice today to invite structure and solitude into your life?

"Solitude is creativity's best friend, and
solitude is refreshment for our souls."

NAOMI JUDD

WHAT'S YOUR STORY?

"The purpose of a storyteller is not to tell you how to think, but to give you questions to think upon."

BRANDON SANDERSON

Almost every time I facilitate a small-group leadership discussion, I ask the team to share some of their story. Predictably, half the group jumps at the opportunity to transparently relay "who" they are and the "story" that informs their lives. It is one of the most powerful moments of any gathering because our story is the truth of where we've been and often the spark of our motivations. Our personal narrative is the essence of who we are and the impetus for how we engage with others.

We all have a story. It explains our past and inspires our future; it is, was, and will always be essential to who we become. As Harvard's Dr. Howard Gardner says, "Stories constitute the single most powerful weapon in a leader's arsenal."[50] The research suggests we almost exclusively operate within a "story mindset." Leaders who are not afraid to enter someone else's story understand the power of empathy. But leaders who are not afraid to share their **OWN** story understand the power of vulnerability. The future belongs to the storytellers.

> We all have a story. It explains our past and inspires our future.

One of the best predictors of professional success isn't likeability, attention to detail, or even industry expertise, but how one authentically tells a story. Most people in sales and marketing work in facts, details, and stats. In doing so, they overwhelm their customers with the weight of information, and it is forgotten as quickly as it is received. Researchers Dan and Chip Heath found that after a presentation 63 percent of attendees remember stories, while only 5 percent remember statistics.[51]

Stories move us—but why?

"Stories create community, enable us to see through the eyes of other people, and open us to the claims of others,"[52] says Peter Forbes, photographer and author. When emotions get too complicated, it is time to rely on a story to simplify the moment. Jimmy Neil Smith, director of the International Storytelling Center, points out that "we are all storytellers. We all live in a network of stories. There isn't a stronger connection between people than storytelling."[53] People with a story can't be ignored.

The pioneering work of neuroeconomics leader Paul Zak has uncovered that storytelling triggers the release of oxytocin, which encourages empathy in the receiver of the story. This release is what researchers refer to as the "trust hormone," a chemical that encourages empathy.[54]

We prefer pictures and relate to stories, not facts. Ironically, facts are oftentimes debatable, but stories allow us to connect with reality. Again, we process visuals sixty thousand times faster than text.[55] A good story speaks to our intellect, our emotions, and our basic psychology.

Business is about relationships. It is about storytelling and connecting my story to yours. So how do we all utilize stories in our professional life? Two ideas to consider:

SHARE PAIN. Do you have the courage to open a discussion sharing how you and your team have failed? This includes the missteps, the confusion, and the frustrations you have encountered. This is much more believable, authentic, and human. If you have finally uncovered an idea worth discussing with your customer, it was more than likely birthed out of quite a lot of pain. Why not share the whole story, not just the boring sanitized version? Now that is a story worth listening to *and remembering*.

WHAT IF? What if all of us are missing something that is right before us? What if, with one decision, we could double our sales, improve loyalty with our customers, and reduce complexity within our lives? What if we could transform a current partnership with one decision?

Effective storytelling oftentimes begins with a question. The right question opens the door for cocreation with your customers and leads you into the future. Stories are journeys, and they oftentimes begin by questioning something. A thoughtful, disruptive "What if?" question sets the stage for a compelling story. It opens the audience to discover.

The best organizations are not afraid of telling stories. As J. R. R. Tolkien shared in a letter to his son, "A story must be told or there'll be no story, yet it is the untold stories that are most moving."[56]

Quit dumping lots of data and tell your untold story. Transport them and take them on a journey.

WHAT NOW?

When does defensiveness show up? What does it cost you, and what one thing can you practice today to better share your personal or company story?

"People think in stories, not statistics."

ARIANNA HUFFINGTON

FEARLESS

"The enemy is fear. We think it is hate, but it is fear."

MAHATMA GANDHI

I remember the first time I had to speak in public. It was in fourth grade, and I felt the walls closing in on me like a horror movie. In eighth grade when I had to answer a question in front of the class, my throat tightened up, and the tension of the moment triggered stuttering. In my first year out of college, a sales training conference caused my knees to shake violently and my voice to tremble uncontrollably. I felt more panicked in that moment than ever before.

I remember in each of those moments feeling out of control, anxious, and fearful of looking foolish. I can think back to those three examples and trigger myself into that uncomfortable state. As I reflect on choices made (or not made), I wonder what pushed me into sales. In retrospect, the sales and eventual management experiences forced me to confront many fears that had always held me back when I was younger.

Uncertainty creates fear, and no one likes uncertainty.

Judith Glaser, author of *Conversational Intelligence*, reminded me that when our certainty is under attack, we can feel neurological pain like that of a physical attack. Glaser states, "When we are out to win at all costs, we operate from the part of the primitive brain called the 'amygdala.'"[57] This is hardwired with the well-developed instincts of fight, flight, freeze, or appease that have evolved over millions of years. When we feel threatened, the amygdala activates the immediate impulses that ensure our survival. Our brain locks down, and we are no longer open to influence. Are you aware of how personal fears hold you back?

When we have conversations with others, our brain maps and subconsciously starts reading the interactions of others. We quickly determine if the person is "safe" or a "threat."

Interestingly, distrust is signaled by one part of the brain and trust by another. Again, we subconsciously compare our expectations of what we think will happen to what does. This difference between expectations and reality is where anxiety and fear kick in. Research shows that when we are relaxed with one another, our heart rate decreases and our brain signals that we are safe.

When we feel unsafe, threatening memories are triggered, and defenses kick in: either fight or flight.

One of the most valuable skills a leader can possess is the ability to have fierce (honest) discussions with others while keeping them safe. When someone feels threatened during a fierce conversation, they immediately begin to protect themselves, fighting back, and losing the ability to stay present in the discussion.

> **One of the most valuable skills ... is the ability to have fierce (honest) discussions with others while keeping them safe.**

Anxiety and fear color how we see reality. Once fear kicks in, we are triggered by memories of pain from the past. Fear is no longer my enemy, but a friend who warns me of danger. If you could harness fear, what could you become?

WHAT NOW?

When do uncertainty and fear show up? What do they cost you, and what one thing can you practice today to increase your feeling of safety?

"And now that you don't have to
be perfect, you can be good."

JOHN STEINBECK

RADICAL CONCENTRATION

"Muddy water, let stand, becomes clear."

LAO TZU

Almost fifteen years ago, I sat on a deserted beach overlooking Lake Michigan and wrote the heart of the playbook that would become Mack Elevation, my consulting, training, and leadership event practice. The idea of bringing together leaders to discuss their journeys, challenges, and growth practices felt like a calling to me, and it changed the direction of my life. This period of reflection generated a blueprint and sense of clarity that still guides me today. There is always the potential to birth something special when we stop to pause, reflect, and go deeper.

> **Our ability to pause and connect new dots is a creative engine we underutilize.**

Our ability to pause and connect new dots is a creative engine we underutilize. But it is the heart of innovation and where art originates. We must allow our unconscious to do what it does best: create!

Productivity expert and researcher Cal Newport explained that the biggest similarity of great creative minds—Twain, Einstein, and even Tolkien—is their habit of finding reclusive work environments. Like them, Newport spends a significant part of his workday in "deep work," a phrase that describes the golden hour of mental productivity when attention is uninterrupted and hyperfocused on the task at hand and immediately dismissed when work is done. As Newport puts it, "If your brain is how you make a living, then you have to worry about cognitive fitness—are you taking care to get good performance out of your brain or not?"[58]

WHY IS STOPPING SO DARN HARD?

Author Jennifer Porter states in an *HBR* article entitled "Why You Should Make Time for Self-Reflection" that the most difficult leaders to coach are those who do not self-reflect. They are not tapping into their creative engine. Porter states, "Reflection gives the brain an opportunity to pause amidst the chaos, untangle and sort through observations and experiences, consider multiple possible interpretations, and create meaning. This meaning becomes learning, which can then inform future mindsets and actions."[59] This is mandatory for creativity.

But the delusion of certainty is ever present. Software product expert turned concentration guru Tristan Harris says that, until one realizes the addictive nature of distraction, the game is rigged against *everyone*. "To be human is to be persuadable at every single moment. The thing about magic, as an example, is that it works on everybody ... It's not about what someone knows, it's about how your mind actually works."[60] Our minds need solitude and momentum to perform, and more than ever before, they're starved of exactly that.

One study by Di Stefano, Gino, Pisano, and Staats found that a group of employees who spent fifteen minutes reflecting on the lessons of that day performed 23 percent better after only ten days.[61] The unfortunate reality is that most of our executives will understand the importance of reflection and simply fail to slow down. A recent study stated that soccer goalies who stay in the center of the goal, instead of diving left or right, have a 33 percent chance of stopping a kicked ball. Yet only 6 percent stay in the middle.[62] We all (like goalies) believe "doing something" is better than stopping and "doing nothing." But we are sadly mistaken. What's stopping you from reflecting more?

WHAT NOW?

When does your lack of self-reflection show up? What does it cost you, and what one thing can you practice today to increase deep work?

"Follow effective action with quiet reflection. From the quiet reflection will come even more effective action."

PETER DRUCKER

SELF-CONTROL IS A SCARCE RESOURCE

"A man who can't bear to share his habits
is a man who needs to quit them."

STEPHEN KING

I have a love/hate relationship with structure and discipline in my life. I push back when others place controls on me, yet I personally coach others on the positive benefits of structure, routines, and rituals. Maybe like you, I deceive myself when I debate the structure others impose on me. Embracing constraints seems to be something we all struggle with at some point. Executive coach and change management expert Marshall Goldsmith reminds us, "Structure is how we overcome depletion. When we have structure, we don't have to make as many choices; we just follow the plan."

Goldsmith believes many of us think we're above using a simple checklist to stay organized, as though "only complexity is worthy of our attention." Goldsmith continues, "We discount structure when it comes to honing our relational behavior. We do not get better without structure. The act of giving and receiving feedback is vital, making us more mindful."[63]

When we have structure and ritual, we take control of our agenda. More control, ironically, gives us more freedom, yet our environment and our history can hinder our rituals and focus. Goldsmith says we forget that "self-control is a limited resource." Epiphanies can occur but typically are short lived because they are based on "impulse" rather than strategy and structure.

When we have structure and ritual, we take control of our agenda.

Goldsmith teaches top leaders the power of utilizing "daily questions." I dare you to try this in your own life. Begin each day with an honest look in the mirror and ask these three questions:

- How are you progressing in your area of focus?

- What's getting in the way of progress?

- Who can help you this week?

The more we practice daily questions, the more it becomes a ritual or routine. Daily questions slow you down, force you to pause, and encourage you to get help. To truly change behavior, create a ritual, and allow others to question you. Change is always difficult. Goldsmith's work reminds us all, "If we do not create and control our environment, our environment creates and controls us. Good behavior is not random; it's logical, it follows a pattern, it's within one's control."

We can't improve without structure. It is how we seize control of an unruly environment. There is no "one size fits all." Answering your own daily or weekly questions offers a scorecard to track progress. The process of having someone you trust ask three questions helps you monitor and control your attention. It creates a winning structure.

We are reminded that the goal is to "establish a set of habits and practices that allow us to respond gracefully to new inputs and to instinctively place our attention where it will be most effective. With that kind of trust and clarity, priorities become irrelevant—we will naturally work on whatever task is most meaningful for us right now."

WHAT NOW?

When do your bad habits show up? What do they cost you, and what one thing can you practice today to build on your rituals, routines, and structure?

"Sow a thought, and you reap an act; Sow an act,
   and you reap a habit; Sow a habit, and you reap a
   character; Sow a character, and you reap a destiny."

SAMUEL SMILES

REFLECTION TIME

1. Does your culture formally (and honestly) conduct lessons learned and self-critique after a project?

2. Are you brave enough to appoint someone to check you on your leadership vulnerabilities?

3. What behavior do you need to forget or unlearn that once served you but no longer does today?

4. Are you ruthless about protecting your calendar, or do you let others control your day?

5. Have previous successes made you vulnerable to a future fall, and where are you at risk?

6. What story are you believing or telling yourself that you must let go of?

7. Are you in the moment with others, or are you teased away to another land?

8. Is your team having fun, and what fears are hindering cohesiveness and impact?

9. What lies or old scripts are holding you back from risking more or being more vulnerable?

10. Do you lead with your mask on, and could you benefit from working with a coach?

RELATIONAL

A common theme throughout this book is the necessity for trust in all relationships. Identifying and exposing personal vulnerability are surefire ways to improve trust within a relationship. When trust is established between two parties, efficiency, growth, and loyalty immediately expand.

Leaders who can ask great questions and listen attentively are able to create cohesive and honest environments within their organizations. Listening is a vital and underappreciated skill in most relationships, but too often, great ideas fall on deaf ears. If you're the leader of a team, practice setting aside judgments or preconceptions and empathetically listen to what is being said (and not said).

Practice setting aside judgments or preconceptions and empathetically listen to what is being said (and not said).

We are relational, and this section will hopefully encourage self-reflection and a critical assessment of how you relate to others. It is also a compilation of ideas, new thinking, and practices shared by leaders within the share groups I facilitated for over a decade. Are you truly aware of how others experience you?

Nobel Prize winner Daniel Kahneman believes there are two distinct methods of thinking. Type 1 thinking is a reactionary, emotional thought process and frequently acts as a shortcut for our brain, while type 2 is a slow and methodical approach to a problem, more resistant to bias, and overall, more rational. The shortcuts within type 1 thinking are called heuristics or internal judgments, and often aid us by allowing quick decision-making to occur through our brain's tendency to see patterns. Heuristics can also be very harmful if left unchallenged.

These interpersonal relationships are especially hindered by unchecked heuristics or blind spots because we find it difficult to honestly assess the way we interact with others. The disconnection felt between people is palpable when it occurs; however, it's often difficult to fully grasp what causes the disconnection. These blind spots are most frequently felt when interacting with others and are most toxic when a leader doesn't realize they're plagued by them. As you go through this section of the book, try to ask yourself this simple question: "How do I affect others?" In this self-analysis, try to slow down and use type 2 thinking to prevent personal biases from getting in the way of the truth.

"No one shows up fully awake. We all suffer from personal blind spots that hinder how we connect with others and how we build relationships. We are not as self-aware as we think."

YOUR TEAM'S
EMOTIONAL HEALTH

"None of us is as smart as all of us."

KEN BLANCHARD

Early in my career, I worked for a manager that celebrated the idea that meetings were an opportunity to test young associates—a moment to "trap and humiliate" and uncover weaker, underperforming employees. He called people out, belittled them in front of peers, and utilized intimation as a core practice of his leadership philosophy. That culture left emotional scars in the hearts and minds of most individuals who survived the job assignment. We've evolved, and workplace laws have improved, but emotionally unhealthy leaders are still everywhere.

Psychologist Robert Hogan claims that 60–75 percent of managers are poor or even incompetent leaders.[64] A recent Gallup poll supports this claim, stating that companies fail to choose the right candidate for the job 82 percent of the time.[65] Most organizations prop up dysfunctional business practices and insecure leaders, damaging the fabric of the culture. A high percentage of leaders are not as emotionally healthy as they think, and their teams are at risk.

Emotionally insecure and fragile managers create dysfunctional teams. Consider this: most professionals switch tasks every three minutes, and interruptions eat up 28 percent of the workday. The research shows that after an interruption, it can take over 23 minutes to get back on task.[66] This leads to a culture of distraction, impulsiveness, and underperformance—all symptoms of an unhealthy team environment. Lack of consistency can spawn uncertainty and self-consciousness within most companies. And this corporate culture reflects the psychological health of the leader.

HOW'S YOUR TEAM'S EMOTIONAL HEALTH?

Organizations are struggling with the pressure of a hypercompetitive workplace, causing high levels of stress and anxiety. A Deloitte external marketplace survey uncovered that nearly 70 percent of employees stated that their employers were not doing enough to prevent or alleviate burnout.[67]

Furthermore, 77 percent of employees said they have experienced employee burnout in their current role. They shared those employers were not creating well-being programs to help alleviate stress in the workplace. Additionally, the survey found that nine of ten people believe high levels of stress or frustration hinder their overall performance.

Stanford professor and economist Jeffrey Pfeffer states, "In a perverse twist, longer work hours have become a status symbol—a marker of how important, indeed indispensable, someone is ... As such, people want to put in long hours to signal how valuable they are."[68] We work too many hours with diminishing returns, sleep with our phones, and miss vital moments with our families. This behavior, rooted in fear, is another sign of dysfunctional leadership.

HAPPY, PRODUCTIVE CULTURES THRIVE.

Shawn Achor served as head teaching fellow at Harvard and designed a course called "Happiness." His work validated something sales leaders experience each day: optimistic sales-people outperform their pessimistic coun-terparts by 56 percent.[69] They help create a positive, creative culture that is fun—or at least not energy draining. The emotions of pessimistic salespeople must be rerouted in today's demanding service culture.

Optimistic managers create high-performing cultures.

The same is true for managers. Optimistic managers create high-performing cultures. One study found that teams with encouraging managers performed 31 percent better than teams whose managers were overly critical. Positive encouragement, it turns out, was even more inspiring than cash payouts. In chaos, an affirmation can be more important than compensation.

The most vibrant organizations are centered on purpose and hope. Annie McKee, author and senior fellow at the University of Pennsylvania's Graduate School of Education, reminds us: "Hope makes it possible to navigate complexity, handle stress, fear, frustration, and understand hectic organizations and lives. Hope, like purpose, positively affects our brain chemistry. Research has shown that when we feel optimistic, our nervous system shifts from fight-or-flight to calm and poised to act."[70] And positive relationships at work boost employee satisfaction by 50 percent.

Are you creating a positive, encouraging organization?

We often believe that a positive culture is a byproduct of high performance. That may occasionally be true, but Shawn Achor has another perspective: "Happiness comes before success."

What are you doing to create a culture of hope?

WHAT NOW?

When does pessimism show up? What does it cost you, and what one thing can you practice today to model thankfulness within your team?

"The secret to teamwork is an outward mindset."

STEVE YOUNG

RUTHLESS TRUST

"If you tell the truth, you don't have to remember anything."

MARK TWAIN

I always flinch when I hear someone in conversation say, "Let me be honest with you." My first thought is, "Why, haven't you been honest all along?" A good friend of mine always enters new relationships with the presupposition that the person they are introduced to is trustworthy until trust is violated. That philosophy is a bit disruptive to me, yet I admire it because it feels so human and hopeful. Trust is the cement that holds relationships and organizations together. When you don't have enough trust, you must rely on control. Control will work for a limited time, but it has an expiration date. Not only is control a much more exhausting process, but it also frequently ends in revolt and failure.

Trust is the cement that holds relationships and organizations together.

In its Global CEO Survey, PwC reported that over half of CEOs think that a lack of trust is a threat to their organization's growth.[71] Lack of trust will always create low retention and difficulty attracting game-changing talent. Trust is the ultimate currency, and it serves as organizational glue. Yet it is rare and fleeting.

Forty percent of Americans find brands and companies less truthful today than twenty years ago, according to research by McCann.[72] Ironically, eight of ten people believe brands have the power to make the world a better place. People want to believe brands and organizations will make a difference, yet rarely are their desires met.

In his recent *HBR* article, "The Neuroscience of Trust," neuroeconomist and founding director of the Center for Neuroeconomics Studies Paul J. Zak reminds us that "employees in high-trust organizations are more productive, have more energy at work, collaborate better with their colleagues, and stay with their employers longer than people working at low-trust companies."[73] His research uncovered that these employees are 50 percent more productive than low-trust organizations. Trust is a catalyst for growth.

We are all lulled into believing humility is synonymous with frailty. But, as Ashley Merryman writes in a recent *Washington Post* article, humility is when we understand our strengths and weaknesses and are *"liberated by this knowledge."*[74] Humble leaders practice staying present and are skilled at neutralizing their own blind spots. They are not afraid to admit their weaknesses.

Researchers Bradley Owens and David Hekman sourced groundbreaking research studying humble leadership across a wide spectrum of fields including the armed services, business, and the clergy. The researchers found humility bolsters a leader's authority, power, and impact. In contrast, nonhumble leaders get their strength from a position of certainty.[75] The nonhumble believe they have all the answers; their need for certainty distracts them and limits their ability to see clearly. Craving clarity, they try to reduce risk, uncertainty, and fear. The better answer is embracing leadership vulnerability, leading to a culture of trust.

Former General Electric CEO Jack Welch once described trust by saying, "I could give you a dictionary definition, but you know it when you feel it."[76] Trusting relationships are the glue of high-performing teams. And if trust is absent, leaders rely on control. "Ruthless trust" is currency, and it's rare.

My research shows three leadership flaws that hinder **ORGANIZATIONAL TRUST**:

1. Leaders often manipulate others, distort facts, set unclear expectations, and spin the truth. Most people see through this, breaking confidence within the team.

2. Leaders often pretend to care about team members. But you can't fake heart; this connection matters for long-term organizational effectiveness. The best teams have created the bond of faithfulness with each other.

3. Leaders often fail to apologize quickly for miscues or operate with little transparency. This leaves them vulnerable. We must lay our cards on the table and encourage ongoing feedback to earn "share of heart" with others. How are you at immediately owning a mistake?

I still don't understand how leaders fail to comprehend that "trust drives productivity." High-trust teams are more engaged, create positive energy, and have a higher employee retention rate. High-trust organizations outperform low-trust firms, every time.

Are you trustworthy?

WHAT NOW?

When does lack of trust show up? What does it cost you, and what one thing can you practice today to promote confidence and trust with others?

"The best way to find out if you can trust
  somebody is to trust them."
                                        ERNEST HEMINGWAY

ARE OTHERS ALLERGIC TO YOUR LEADERSHIP STYLE?

"Talent wins games, but teamwork and
 intelligence win championships."

MICHAEL JORDAN

"He doesn't listen to others … He gets so defensive when others share improvement ideas with him." And "he doesn't give enough positive feedback to associates throughout the year." Each of these three statements were taken out of personal interviews I conducted with peers of a new client prior to beginning our coaching relationship. When I shared some of these verbatim comments, he was shocked and crushed. I reminded him that none of us are the leader we think we are. It's a hard pill to swallow, but all the research points in that direction. In fact, as we enjoy more success, we receive less honest feedback, becoming disengaged from reality. In addition, we often don't ask for feedback nor set a safe atmosphere for others to share it. Self-reflection is distorted when we create these echo chambers.

Psychologist and author Heidi Grant Halvorson states, "One of the things we have learned from over 50 years of research on perception is that most of the time, we assume other people see us the way we see ourselves. A second thing we've learned is that that is almost never true."[77]

In my coaching and training practice, I have uncovered seven wicked leadership dysfunctions that hinder our overall effectiveness:

THE SEVEN:

1. Overestimating yourself and underestimating others.

2. The need to be right instead of doing what's right.

3. Not listening or being present with others.

4. Making everything high priority versus the critical few.

5. Too much selfish ambition.

6. Not being honest about others' performance.

7. Too much stake in the past as an indicator of the future.

No matter how you cover them up, they eventually leak out. And the more you deny or bury them, the worse they become.

Here is the dirty little secret: everyone already sees your weaknesses and would respect you even more if you owned them and opened up about how you confront them.

Everyone already sees your weaknesses and would respect you even more if you owned them.

As we have discussed in the past, it's crucial to embrace the growth mindset. As Dr. Carol Dweck says, "People who must look good, or people who think mistakes are bad, or people who dislike accountability have a hard time learning things."[78]

In other words, failing to embrace your weaknesses or blind spots can be lethal to your long-term impact. Three ideas to consider:

1. Work with a trusted performance coach who is strong enough to pull out your best but also confront you about your worst. Others may admire your strengths, but they will never forget your worst moments. Are you courageous enough to work with a coach?

2. Gain ongoing insights from a "No B.S. Buddy" who is always ruthlessly honest with you. Confidants that share the unfiltered truth are your most valuable advocates. Have you given a trusted friend permission to critique your performance in real time?

3. Slow down, pause, and listen until it hurts. We now live in a culture that is addicted to activity and does not value thoughtful reflection. You cannot see clearly unless you learn to slow down and consider how you are impacting others and the quality of your decisions. Are you committed to being more thoughtful?

Learning new skills is exciting, but unlearning leadership behaviors that no longer serve you will set you apart. Learn to approach your personal development with a "beginner's mind."

WHAT NOW?

When does self-centeredness show up? What does it cost you, and what one thing can you practice today to embody selflessness?

"No matter how brilliant your mind or strategy, if you're playing a solo game, you'll always lose out to a team."

REID HOFFMAN

THE HABITS OF EXCEPTIONAL PARTNERSHIPS

"Remember, teamwork begins by building trust. And the only way to do that is to overcome our need for invulnerability."

PATRICK LENCIONI

One of the most common things I tell people in coaching sessions is to embrace transparency. This insight was learned growing up in a family coping with alcoholism. You realize that transparency keeps you honest and helps you build stronger relationships with others. We all go through life portraying an idealized version of ourselves, concealing weaknesses, and being dishonest about how we are doing. Hiding behind your mask creates problems that are often hard to pinpoint because they are obscured by layers of fear and insecurities.

Every second matters when a relationship crisis arises or a problem is uncovered. Bluntly and transparently telling a partner about how you're doing is always better than the sugar-coated alternative, which feels good in the moment but will inevitably lead to conflict. Are you candid and truthful with your peers, associates, and partners?

Honesty and empathy are the lifeblood of the best relationships. Knowing you can count on a partnership provides fluidity in even the most turbulent times. When lightning strikes, mutually beneficial and codeveloped solutions to problems are too often replaced by a mindset of self-preservation. We start to view our relationships exclusively as outlets for personal gain instead of a connection that requires ongoing cultivation. Why is it that most relationships dissolve due to insufficient transparency and trust, becoming simply transactional? The best partnerships are cemented by shared risk and mutual investment, enriched by clear and healthy dialogue between both parties.

How would you grade the quality of your partnerships with your top customers? Does your team outperform more than half of your competitors? Are you perceived as the standard in your sector? Bain & Company surveyed over three hundred companies and discovered that 80 percent of companies describe their service experience as "superior," while only 8 percent of customers saw it that way.[79] That perception gap is frightening and sobering. We often think we are more competitive than we really are, and that is why it's essential to always think like a start-up: question everything.

At a recent leadership event I moderated, the group members discussed insights detailed in a Bain Report, *Barriers and Pathways to Sustainable Growth: Harnessing the Power of the Founder's Mentality.* The report found 85 percent of executives believed internal barriers, not external, were the primary obstacles to growth.[80] The research emphasized that revenue growing faster than talent acquisition, erosion of accountability, and loss of mission are substantial factors hindering growth. Many of today's top organizations including Google, Apple, Amazon, and Netflix institutionally embrace a start-up mentality. That psychology is part of the magic of their culture.

So, what are the new rules for creating healthy, vibrant partnerships in any industry? My research has shown that only one in seven companies ever ascend to the level of strategic partner with their customers. The strongest strategic partnerships have some similar characteristics:

1. They share uncommon trends bubbling up on the fringe and prioritize "What's next?" questions.

2. They have an insatiable curiosity, listen intently, and possess a granular understanding of customer needs.

3. They align on mutual goals and courageously attack challenges together.

4. They operate with a healthy obsession, questioning themselves and taking nothing for granted.

5. They practice full transparency and do not pull back from difficult conversations.

6. They think holistically, understanding their partner's unstated needs or dreams.

7. They embrace agility and focus on solving unmet needs quicker than competitors.

8. They simplify discussions, recognizing there's value in being concise.

We are all looking for empathetic partners. The ability to transport yourself into another's shoes and understand their needs accurately and precisely is akin to a superpower when used correctly. Many times, people will tell you what you are trying to figure out if you just listen for it. The problem is nobody is listening. People correlate talking with influence, but the truth is, real strength lies in the ability to effectively listen and assess the needs of another. I have noticed in my own practice that most leaders do not understand their customers' needs.

Real strength lies in the ability to effectively listen and assess the needs of another.

According to research by McKinsey, 70 percent of the buying experience is based on how the customer feels they are being treated.[81] Partnerships are rooted in this same insight.

Can you concisely pinpoint your partner's needs, and do they understand yours?

WHAT NOW?

When does your lack of transparency show up? What does it cost you, and what one thing can you practice today to strengthen your partnerships?

"No one can whistle a symphony. It
takes a whole orchestra to play it."

H. E. LUCCOCK

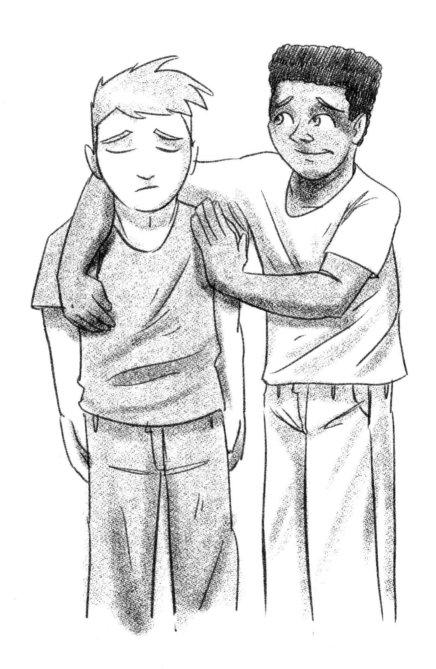

EMPATHY IS YOUR THIRD EYE

"Courage starts with showing
up and letting ourselves be seen."

BRENÉ BROWN

Comedians have a third eye. This eye allows them the empathy to see things and comprehend human motivation on a deeper human level. Robin Williams overflowed with empathy, embodying characters who were especially gifted at invoking emotion in a matter of minutes. Empathy is not just a soft skill; it's the force behind every healthy team. Empathetic people have the unique ability to stand firmly in another's shoes, feeling what they feel. As novelist Mohsin Hamid shared, "Empathy is about finding echoes of another person in yourself."

The devaluation of empathy in our culture has created a crisis of indifference where people struggle to find connection to one another. When coaches do not practice empathy, they fail to tap into the unique attributes of their team, and relationships begin to diminish. It starts to break down because both parties fail to understand the other's emotions, motives, and personal story. They have forgotten to properly acknowledge the self-evident idea that everyone's lived experience is different, and we should seek to expand our knowledge of those experiences.

Empathy acts as a bridge between two parties, opening lines of communication previously locked. If empathy is championed within a relationship, then there's a mutual understanding of each other's fears, needs, and goals. "When two countries have high levels of connection between them, they're more likely to cooperate and achieve a mutually beneficial agreement; the same can be said of empathy's role within a relationship,"[82] says entrepreneur and innovator Scott Galloway.

Opening the lines of communication and relating to another's needs should be the endgame for leaders. If done correctly, empathy transforms *your* problems into *our* problems and allows for those issues to be dealt with quickly and efficiently.

> **Opening the lines of communication and relating to another's needs should be the endgame for leaders.**

HOW DO YOU USE MORE EMPATHY, AND WHY IS IT SO HARD? Identifying empathy's role in a relationship is the easy part, practicing empathy is where people have difficulty. Author Brené Brown states, "Empathy is a choice, and it is a vulnerable choice because in order to connect with you, I have to connect with something in myself that knows that feeling ... What makes something better is connection ... **EMPATHY FUELS CONNECTION.**"[83] Ask yourself these questions and take a moment to calibrate where you feel like you stand.

DO YOU PRACTICE CURIOSITY IN ALL DISCUSSIONS? Find out "what makes them tick"—especially those most unlike ourselves. Philosopher Roman Krznaric reminds us to observe the natural curiosity of children and model their inquisitiveness, learning to question everything. "Curiosity expands our empathy when we talk to people outside our usual social circle, encountering lives and world views very different from our own."[84] Curiosity expands context, broadening our scope and building empathy.

DO YOU LISTEN WITH VULNERABILITY, OR DO YOU SUCK UP THE OXYGEN IN THE ROOM? People with high levels of empathy listen to others on an emotional level. They are not afraid to be vulnerable with those who disagree, creating fervent bonds that encourage honest conversation. Vulnerability and empathy light the fire of creativity.

HOW SOCIALLY SENSITIVE ARE YOU? The very best teams are experts at reading the nonverbals, voice fluctuations, and expressions of their companions. In other words, strong emotional intelligence and sensitivity toward teammates' feelings are the corner-stones of a strong team.

Most teams are resistant to using empathy because it forces groups to be fearlessly unguarded. If a team leader is unable or unwilling to create a safe culture where people can voice concerns, then the culture will instead be ruled by fear and conformity.

Diversity of thought on a team is paramount yet fragile if unpro-tected. Do you truly understand others around you?

WHAT NOW?

When does your lack of empathy show up? What does it cost you, and what one thing can you practice today to convey understanding to others?

"Imperfections are not inadequacies; they are reminders that we're all in this together."

BRENÉ BROWN

ARE YOU A MICROMANAGER?

"Micromanagement is the destroyer of momentum."

MILES ANTHONY SMITH

No one ever wants to be considered an oppressive person. Most people who struggle with micromanagement don't readily admit that they control others. Micromanagement, like any other compulsion, is rooted in control, weakness, and fear. This is a fear of losing control, of looking bad, of feeling less than, or of failure. I once had a younger manager on my team that demanded perfection on every report, presentation, and business meeting. It was difficult to observe and was tyrannical to her associates. After a few months, I asked her a very provocative question. I asked, "What are you compensating for with all this demand for perfection?" Her eyes watered up, and it opened her up to a vulnerable two-hour personal conversation that shifted her in a new direction in leading her team.

An organization strangled by a controlling leader will never realize its full potential. Smothering, controlling leaders limit creativity, self-

> **An organization strangled by a controlling leader will never realize its full potential.**

expression, and innovative thinking. Here is a clue. If someone says, "I am not trying to micromanage," then they probably are.

Have others in your sphere ever told you that you are guilty of:

- Intervening too often, using too many tracking forms, or holding too many meetings.

- Setting too many objectives or having an inability to admit mistakes, show weaknesses, or receive feedback.

- Always having to uncover miscues, mistakes, or errors of others.

Employees quit managers, not companies. The research is very compelling, convicting, and conclusive. Over three quarters of employees say their manager creates the culture at work, and over half say they have left a job because of their manager.[85] Yet healthy managers make all the difference. Over half of employees also stated they would start a job with a lower salary if that meant working for a great boss.[86] A toxic manager can demotivate and push people out the door, and a healthy, encouraging leader may just be your best employee retention asset.

Micromanagers suffer from internal fear. Most of the time, this behavior is rooted in deep-seated insecurities. If this is you, you are not alone, but this strategy scares the best talent away. You frustrate others and probably blame them instead of looking in the mirror. You may present a Teflon image, but you know the truth.

Management is doing things right; leadership is doing the right things, said Peter Drucker. Leaders that thrive are very adaptable. They possess multiple communication styles, allowing them to optimize their personal and professional associations depending on the circumstance.

They build relationships to get the best out of each relationship. When they are working with action-oriented people, they are very concise and to the point. With logical or disciplined mates, they are very linear in their communications. And with high-vision people, they utilize stories and cast a vision to optimize the discussion.

They don't just rely on control to create an outcome; they adapt their personal style to best align with and support the needs of the individual based on the person's preference. They are very flexible or versatile, and control is *not* one of their communication styles. Great teams are ecosystems: communal, service-oriented, inspired by vision, and empowered toward change.

WHAT NOW?

When does fear of losing control show up? What does it cost you, and what one thing can you practice today to empower others?

"The "result" of micromanagement is perhaps tangible in the short run, but more often causes damage for the long term."

PEARL ZHU

WHO STEALS YOUR ENERGY?

"I can't give you a surefire formula for success,
 but I can give you a formula for failure: try
 to please everybody all the time."

HERBERT BAYARD SWOPE

Early in my career, I was coached on building my time management skills, but today I believe the better question is: "Who steals your energy?" When I am honest about days that get away from me, the culprit is dysfunctional people who tap my spirit, stamina, and energy. Our energy is finite, vital to creativity, and demands boundaries. Energy needs to be protected and distributed to people, projects, and ideas that are deserving. Not everyone values nor *deserves* your energy.

A recent Boston Consulting Group article authored by Roselinde Torres, Peter Tolman, Susie Grehl, and Eva Sage-Gavin argues that "CEOs who harness energy accelerate value creation, while those who deplete energy or allow it to dissipate struggle to achieve their goals."[87]

Your energy is the lifeblood that sets the tone for every encounter, and it's the influence

Energy animates a culture and everyone within it.

that runs through any organization. Energy is not a thermometer measuring temperature; it's a thermostat that sets the temperature and tone for a group. Energy animates a culture and everyone within it. What does the research say about energy?

IT'S CONTAGIOUS. Whatever your energy level, it's deposited onto others. It leaves an imprint and an impact. Want to decipher the energy of a team? Look at the leader. Are you aware of how others receive your energy? All leaders are (for lack of a better term) chief energy officers, imbuing either anxiety or calmness in times of stress.

IT'S CREATION. It allows people to better engage with each other. The research shows that positive energy encourages risk taking, greater productivity, purpose and invigoration, momentum, and adaptability, while expanding everyone's capacities. It is the ultimate growth mindset.

IT'S CHOREOGRAPHY. We must deliberately protect (and map) our energy by taking control of our calendar. If you are not building in energy-recovery activities throughout the day or setting healthy boundaries (especially when traveling), you're losing energy and may not even know. Are you allowing others to zap you? What are your daily rituals that disperse stress?

How do you evaluate energy drain?

Tony Schwartz, an expert on energy management, asks the question, "Are you heading for an energy crisis?"[88] His teachings emphasize awareness of moments that drain you, while installing and staying committed to rituals that replenish your personal energy.

What are the activities and people who steal your energy?

Meetings do not have to be long to be productive. The research says longer meetings are poorer meetings. Schwartz recommends practicing shorter (more impactful) meetings and allowing people to get home early and renew themselves. Are you strong enough to take his advice?

What is your sweet spot for peak performance? Once you understand it, commit to creating an environment where it occurs more often. Multitasking is still the biggest lie in business today. It steals your energy, damages your relationships, hinders your focus, and limits opportunities to go deeper with a subject. Practice narrowing your focus, one task at a time.

Energy is a finite resource. Protect it.

WHAT NOW?

What drains your energy? What does it cost you, and what one thing can you practice today to prioritize life-giving activities?

"Each of us has a finite reservoir of energy in any given day."

TONY SCHWARTZ

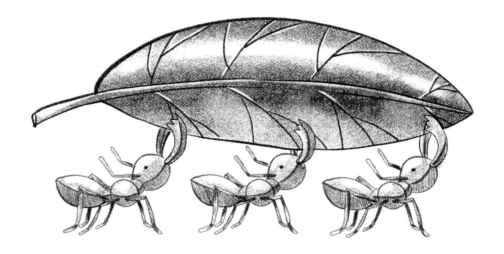

HOLISTIC NEGOTIATIONS

"Trust always affects two outcomes: speed and cost. When trust goes down, speed goes down and cost goes up."

STEPHEN M. R. COVEY

During one of my recent leadership share groups, I noticed that almost every company in the room struggled with the same challenge. Their most important partners and customers are narrowly focused on short-term results, not long-term relationships and mutual gain. Simultaneously, most of the top companies are investing in higher-level negotiation training, and the end results are more tension, frustration, and relationship angst. It's natural to lose track of your script and become bogged down in the transactional nature of some relationships, but it's essential to remember the humanity of the other party. Mutually beneficial negotiations create a sense of trust that carries into the future.

The literature shows that the best relationships are rooted in "seeking to understand" another's agenda with higher-level diplomacy, shared interests, and cocreation. Recently, I conducted research with a group of senior sales leaders that focused on the health of their retail partnerships. The objective of this survey was to uncover the factors hindering their engagements and the profitability with their largest partners. I discovered that one-third of the manufacturers surveyed are struggling with profitability, desire more access to their top customers, and are looking for more creativity from these customers. How do you think your organization is fairing?

Historically, most organizations have taught "technique" negotiation skills, emphasizing "winning" versus creating joint value together. My research shows that many of the top growth organizations do something very different. They uncover hidden challenges (or threats) that their business partners are too close to see. Moreover, they protect the relationship with their partners and offer invaluable insights, addressing the unstated needs of the customer.

I spoke with a group of B2B manufacturers about the most valuable skills they are utilizing in their customer negotiations. Each skill is rooted in creating "win-win" outcomes, not "win-lose." They operate like this, or it is "no deal." If both parties don't feel they have achieved the outcome that benefits them both, they continue working on the deal until both are satisfied. This philosophy is unique in today's transactional world.

Cambridge Negotiations Lab believes there are three key tensions that exist within all negotiations:[89]

1. the tension between creating and distributing value

2. the tension between the interests of principals and their agents

3. the tension between empathizing with another's point of view while asserting your own

An effective negotiator creates mutual value for both parties and sets an atmosphere to navigate difficult discussions. They understand another person's views, unstated needs, values, and preferences, creating a dynamic interpersonal relationship. Five skills differentiate the best negotiators from the rest:

UNSTATED NEEDS. They have a deep understanding of their partner's personal and professional goals, competitive threats, higher-level corporate priorities, and deeper unstated needs. They spend an enormous amount of time diagnosing the landscape and context of the customer. The best will take the time to understand all the reasons for the other's behavior.

An effective negotiator creates mutual value for both parties and sets an atmosphere to navigate difficult discussions.

WHAT IF? Prior to all important customer meetings, they have already thought through the list of concessions they are willing to make during a face-to-face discussion. They are adept at prioritizing the highest value, low-cost tradeable giveaways and the value they want in return.

HYPERDISCIPLINE. They eliminate irrelevant topics and maintain a hyperdisciplined meeting outline, speaking less and listening more, and including awareness of nonverbal communication cues. Empathy is not a sales technique; it's a relationship philosophy. It's critical to get inside the head (and heart) of your partner and look for new ways to address their agenda.

UNCOMFORTABLE. One of the biggest mistakes of negotiation is the need to eliminate the feeling of discomfort due to competitive pressures, price demands, deadlines, and combativeness in a buyer/seller discussion. Negotiation pressures can cause us to concede too quickly and hinder our ability to stay present. Get comfortable being uncomfortable.

INTANGIBLE ASSETS. Too often, we tend to settle versus asking for more value and believing we deserve it. What valuable intangible assets does your partner possess that you value and would not be costly to your negotiation partner? We need to clearly understand the intangibles. Words to live by: "It's not the minimum you need but the maximum you deserve."

Negotiation is about understanding how we solve others' problems and what pain we are taking away. It's not about winning; it's about creating mutual value.

Remember, we are all irrational and impulsive—practice staying in the moment.

WHAT NOW?

When does your impulsiveness show up? What does it cost you, and what one thing can you practice today to accentuate win-win discussions?

"No matter how brilliant your mind or strategy, if you're playing a solo game, you'll always lose out to a team."

REID HOFFMAN

FIERCE CONVERSATIONS

"Being aware of your fear is smart.
Overcoming it is the mark of a successful person."

SETH GODIN

Most people have a fear of embracing difficult conversations, and it's easy to understand why most avoid these painful moments. Most people have lost friendships or relationships with family members due to an inability to navigate difficult discussions. I would estimate three of four leaders do not confront their boss when their relationship is deteriorating, and just as many are not completely truthful with their customers. And it gets more personal: a study released by leadership development and conversation experts at Fierce, Inc. finds that toxic employees continue to create headaches in the workplace.[90] However, instead of confronting these difficult employees, over half of everyone avoids these confrontations. The ability to embrace a problematic conversation and navigate it with grace is vital for the health of any relationship.

> **The ability to embrace a problematic conversation and navigate it with grace is vital for the health of any relationship.**

Research fielded by Globis and PDC Consulting highlights that 53 percent of managers report avoiding difficult conversations because they lack the training, experience, and confidence in handling such situations.[91] A large majority of these leaders are seriously concerned about the stress created and an angry response from the person they are confronting.

"Our lives succeed or fail one conversation at a time," states author Susan Scott. "The conversation is the relationship. If the conversation stops, all of the possibilities for the relationship become smaller and all of the possibilities for the individuals in the relationship become smaller." We must all learn to practice fierce conversations—taking off the mask and getting to the root of the emotions or challenges with another person. It requires risk but is an essential leadership skill.

THE COURAGE TO FACE REALITY

We all struggle with sharing difficult news with people in our lives, fearing alienation or damaging important relationships. When we practice sharing reality, we build deeper, more trusting relationships. Scott shares the three phases of facing reality with another person:

1. Identify the issue and proposed solution.

2. Validate that you understand everyone's perspectives and assumptions.

3. Check for agreement, and gather everyone's input.

COME OUT FROM HIDING

It is difficult to speak candidly in a partnership when discussions have become toxic or if trust has been broken. That's why we often dodge the conversation altogether.

If you find yourself not confronting the truth with someone, you may have given away your power. You must be willing to dig deep, protecting the relationship while creating a safe space. The anatomy of a healthy discussion includes:

- Name the issue – be concise and get to the root of the problem and what you've learned.

- Describe it – share your emotions about the issue and how it affects you.

- Clarify what is at stake – identify your contribution to this problem and the ideal outcome.

- Indicate your wish to resolve the issue – ask your partner to respond and share thoughts.

Susan Scott reminds us that "in any situation, the person who can most accurately describe reality without laying blame will emerge as the leader, whether designated or not."[92]

Are you courageous enough to confront your most difficult relationships?

WHAT NOW?

When does your lack of courage show up? What does it cost you, and what one thing can you practice today to embody directness with others?

"Burnout doesn't occur because we're solving problems; it occurs because we've been trying to solve the same problem over and over. The problem named is the problem solved."

SUSAN SCOTT

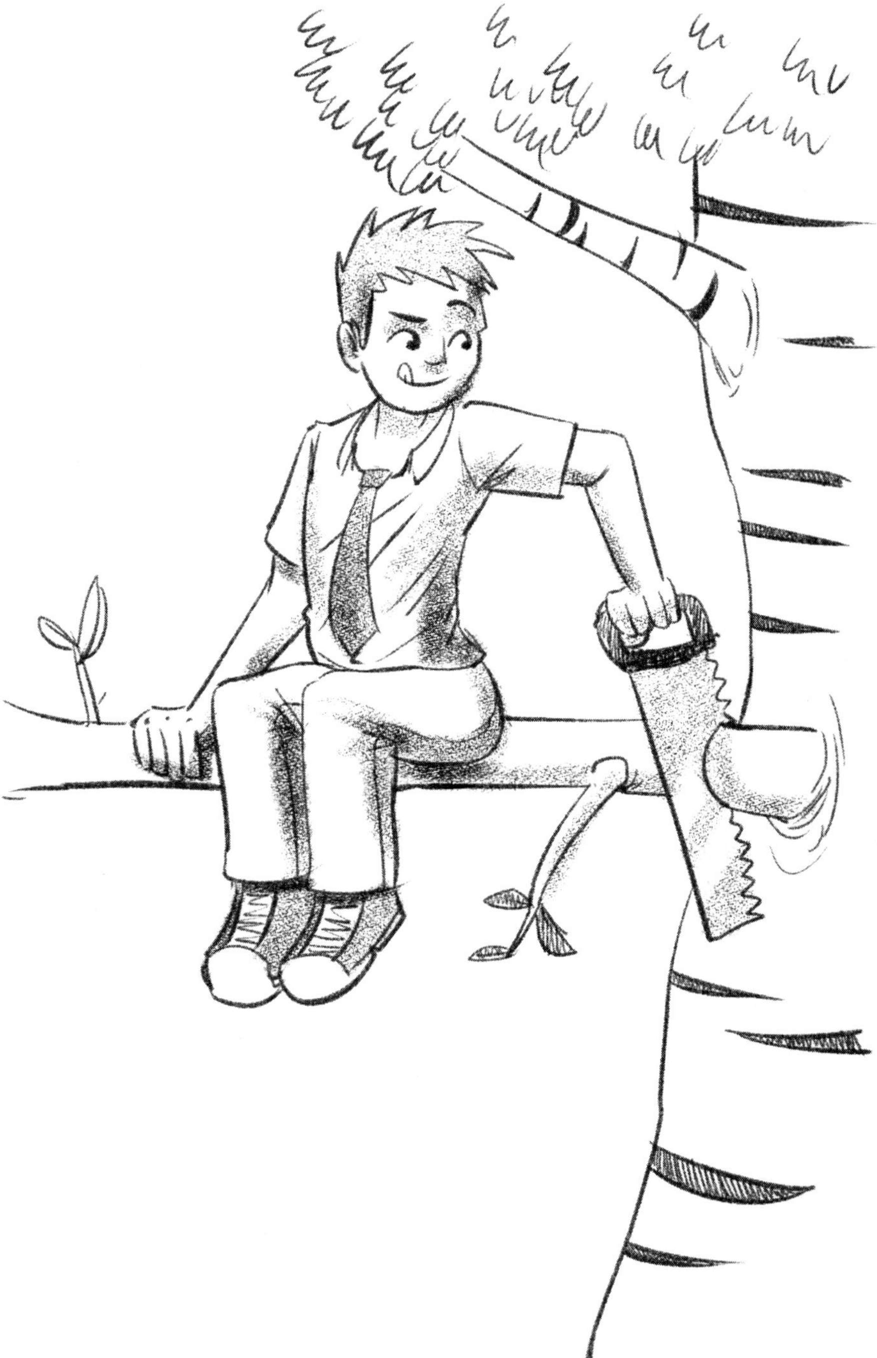

THE SEVEN LAPSES IN JUDGMENT

"For there to be betrayal, there would have to have been trust first. "

SUZANNE COLLINS

I often collaborate with sales and marketing groups to help them understand how to build high-performing teams and collaborate with each other. These two groups are comprised of individuals who possess different skills, temperaments, and often diverse objectives. There are numerous reasons why these two groups have historically had difficulties aligning interests, and they often speak right past each other. During a recent sales and marketing team workshop, a senior-level marketing leader abruptly rolled her eyes at the vice president of sales and barked out, "Your team are always complaining about the marketing plans, and you don't focus enough on your sales objectives. You do sales, and we will do marketing." The gauntlet had been thrown down, and the marketing leader had demonstrated a real lapse in judgment; sales and marketing departments must operate as one to achieve the highest mutual potential.

Do your best customers trust the sales and marketing leaders within your organization? According to the *Journal of Personal Selling*

& Sales Management, 49 percent of surveyed sales managers shared that their sales organizations have lied on calls, and 34 percent have sales teams that made unrealistic promises.[93] Untrustworthy behaviors have a bad poker face. More times than not, the intent, integrity, and results of sales teams get questioned—and with good reason. Are you and your team predictable?

Untrustworthy behaviors have a bad poker face.

According to Tomas Chamorro-Premuzic, professor of business psychology at University College London, "Being trustworthy is in the eye of the beholder, it is a matter of degree, and it is what others think—not you."[94] When someone is perceived as unpredictable, inconsistent, and guarded, they will have trust problems. If you are inconsistent, people will notice.

My research leads me to believe there are seven traps (or lapses in judgment) creating the level of unpredictability that chips away at trust:

1. Not understanding the client's hidden internal needs, interests, or challenges.

2. Giving a presentation vs. moderating a cocreation discussion, designing a custom solution.

3. Using annoying, condescending techniques like leading questions, restatements, and false listening.

4. Failing to recognize mistakes, current problems, risks, or competitors' advantages.

5. Pushing your own ideas even though they do not align with the client's larger "stated" needs.

6. Believing that your solution, service, or product is distinct, even though you are not that different.

7. Thinking you are trying to meet the client's needs—but focusing on your own internal needs.

We all want to see consistency within our family, friends, and sales teams. So how do we eliminate our own inconsistencies and in turn create a perception of reliability? The answer starts with extreme self-awareness and humility. It requires a willingness to ask others one simple question: "How do I affect others?" We normally default to protecting ourselves, but this question unlocks our own self-deceptions and relationship blind spots.

Conveying vulnerability and approachability sets the tone for effective trust building. But research also states that to maintain trust, one must blend credibility, competence, and results.[95] Actions matter more than words. Organizations, politicians, religious leaders, and sales executives are judged on if their promises are kept. The root problem with trust is inconsistency; the cure is consistency (keeping promises).

Do you know how your associates and customers experience you?

WHAT NOW?

When does lack of judgment show up? What does it cost you, and what one thing can you practice today to repair a broken relationship?

"If you are untrustworthy, people will not trust you."

LAO TZU

THE ART OF DISAGREEING

"Be who you are and say what you feel, because those who mind don't matter, and those who matter don't mind."

BERNARD M. BARUCH

How do you engage with or disagree with an overbearing know-it-all? We have all been cornered at a party by a swaggering, overconfident windbag that has opinions on everything and is not interested in conversation, only his monologue. Recently, I was introduced to a senior marketing leader who stole the moment from the room, droning on about his recent CrossFit successes and his unrequested political views. After thirty minutes and the start of a headache, I had to leave the room for a breath of fresh air. His poor self-awareness and even poorer listening skills were off the charts. That evening I failed to redirect the conversation and was unsuccessful in confronting many of his questionable statements. What were my lessons learned?

"Know-it-alls" are disruptive and difficult to manage, and they struggle with both collaboration and feedback. They are addicted to the emotions of trying to impress others with their intelligence. They are also often not team players, can be closed minded and opinionated, and view the world exclusively from their perspective. Simply stated, their insecurities and lack of self-awareness hinder and limit their effectiveness. This is a critical weakness, is dysfunctional, and is growing at epidemic levels.

When you "one-up" or try too hard to impress, your actions depress creativity, fluidity, and candor. The need to be perceived as the smartest person in the room unleashes a backlash of avoidance, frustration, and escape. Think about it: when another is taking up all the oxygen, it's time to leave the room.

Most people talk past and at each other. There is excessive debate and very limited influence when people talk past or at each other. The art of thoughtful critique is rarely found. In philosopher Daniel C. Dennett's book *Intuition Pumps and Other Tools for Thinking*, he poses the question: "Just how charitable are you supposed to be when criticizing the views of an opponent?"[96] Or in other words, how do you get someone to quit talking *at* you and instead talk *to* you?

How do you oppose or criticize someone's view in a healthy manner? Dennett developed an amazing communication model worthy of consideration for our personal and professional life.

STEP 1: Express and restate the person's position so accurately, calmly, and clearly that they could say, "Thanks; I wish I'd thought of putting it that way."

STEP 2: Convey points of agreement that you share with the person.

STEP 3: Share with the person what you "learned" from the discussion.

STEP 4: Only then do you thoughtfully share your rebuttal, opposition, or criticism. Open your counter by sharing "why" you support a different perspective based on your own personal experiences.

Dennett reminds us that this approach creates a safe place for two people to deeply discuss their areas of disagreement, elevating the conversation and allowing for better understanding.

Social psychologist and researcher Alex Huynh reminds us that "distancing tactics, such as trying to see a conflict from a third-person perspective, makes you more likely to reinterpret negative events and find closure."[97] Otherwise, we are more likely to keep reliving similar conflicts.

The global leadership and research agency Potential Project suggests that practicing mindfulness helps us become "less reactive and more proactive." They have discovered that a "diligent approach to mindfulness can help people create a one-second mental space between an event or stimulus and their response to it."[98] It is a "one-second lead over our mind, emotions, and world." And one second is all you need to pause and concentrate on what is being said to you.

Mindfulness and the conversational pause allow the brain to slow down and block out the reactionary fight-or-flight response that is too often used when we feel threatened. Mindfulness allows for the needed pause to neutralize the part of the brain that can trigger a fight-or-flight or a knee-jerk reaction to a perceived threat. It also encourages stronger *executive functioning, poise,* and *peacefulness,* allowing for impulse control.

One second is all you need to talk with someone, not at them.

WHAT NOW?

When does your opposition to others' ideas show up? What does it cost you, and what one thing can you practice today to be inclusive?

"The difference between stupidity and genius is
that genius has its limits."

ALBERT EINSTEIN

LISTEN UNTIL IT HURTS

"You cannot truly listen to anyone and do anything else at the same time."

M. SCOTT PECK

One of my mentors shared with me, "Arguing is a waste of energy because you either come off as hard-headed or incompetent." My friend was right, the answer to most communication challenges is not more talking, but the art of deep listening. The research is abundantly clear: most adult listeners are preoccupied, distracted, and forgetful nearly 75 percent of the time. Most people try to create a positive impression by filling the room with words and expressing what they know. They give monologues and fail to share the floor with other participants. They're asleep at the wheel and don't realize that other team members have mentally exited.

The most impactful people I know are gifted listeners. They let the conversation breathe. They're passionate listeners and thoughtful questioners, and their nonverbal communication cues encourage deeper discussion. Listening should never be a passive action. It involves emotionally connecting and reflecting on what is said and not being said. Active, empathetic listening is a discipline on par with strategy development, marketing acumen, and financial management skills.

Why is listening so underdeveloped?

It's easy to forget that listening is an immersive experience. It is our ability to take in another's body language, tonality, and the full spectrum of nonverbal communication. We forget to not only listen, but listen fully, appreciating context, facial expressions, gestures, voice pitch, and levels of eye contact. When we are not present, we do not "listen between the lines." And unstated communication is oftentimes much more informative than what is stated. If you miss the body language, you have missed the message.

Philosopher Henri Nouwen states, "Somewhere we know that without silence, words lose their meaning, that without listening, speaking no longer heals, that without distance, closeness cannot cure."[99] You will never optimize your business or personal relationships unless you allow for space to listen to the heart of another person. Are you truly staying present with others?

Most people are not encouraged nor recognized for their listening skills, and too often, great listeners are categorized as weak or not assertive. Nothing could be further from the truth. People with adept listening skills are silently assessing and are highly attuned to the people in their lives.

> **You will never optimize your business or personal relationships unless you allow for space to listen to the heart of another person.**

Only 2 percent of people have ever had any formal education on how to listen. Most of us listen at a rate of 125–250 words per minute, but we think at 1,000–3,000 words per minute—creating a deficit in communication. With an economy drowning in content, it's no wonder we are forced to think faster and listen less, leading to new levels of misunderstanding.

I have noticed three reoccurring, negative listening habits that derail most people:

- They assume they understand another's intent without verifying and checking it out.

- They formulate responses prior to an individual completing their thoughts.

- They emotionally shut down because of insecurities versus asking clarifying questions.

Leaders with great influence are professional listeners. They practice asking for and setting an atmosphere that encourages honest feedback. Their teams are comprised of people who align with the vision but are given permission to openly dissent. The most respected leaders I know listen until it hurts.

Remember, listening is immersive and takes time. Listening is participative, relentless, and assertive. It is a skill grounded in empathy and mastered through humility.

The most thoughtful, insightful people I know are gifted listeners. Do you listen to respond, or do you listen to understand?

WHAT NOW?

When do your wrongful assumptions show up? What do they cost you, and what one thing can you practice today to exhibit empathetic listening skills?

"There's a lot of difference between listening and hearing."

G. K. CHESTERTON

A PERFECT QUESTION

"My only weapon is the question."

JORGE RAMOS

Isidor Rabi, Nobel Prize winner in physics, once shared, "My mother made me a scientist. Every other mother in Brooklyn would ask her child after school: 'So? Did you learn anything today?' Not my mother. She always asked me a different question. 'Izzy,' she would say, 'did you ask a good question today?' That difference made me a scientist."[100]

People who question norms are often minimized, attacked, or shut out of the conversation altogether. This happens in politics, religious traditions, and in every facet of culture. Those who dare to ask tough questions, uncovering innovative ideas and confronting old paradigms, are rarely admired for this trait. And yet, new questions (not monologues) answer most challenging situations. Philosopher Peter Abelard stated, "The master key of knowledge is, indeed, a persistent and frequent questioning."[101]

Recently, I moderated a "Customer Acceleration Planning Meeting." I was reminded that questions unlock doors. During our "deep dive" evaluation of the customer's priorities, I noticed five questions that changed the atmosphere of our planning meeting:

1. What is too close to see objectively anymore?

2. Let's assume we are not the best; where are we vulnerable?

3. Where have we lost our distinct advantage?

4. Are we playing scared, and why?

5. What are we not paying attention to that may matter more than we think?

HAVE YOU LOST THE PLOT?

Filmmaker, screenwriter, and director Robert Altman once stated, "The role of the director is to create a space where the actors and actresses can be more than they have ever been before, more than they have ever dreamed of being."[102] The best directors ask questions, uncovering the inner voice of their talent. It always starts with a question: a what, who, or why that forces everyone to return to the plot and understand their role in it.

Organizations that graciously invest in human capital deliver stock market returns *five times higher* than those who are stingy in their talent investment. The research also uncovered that when organizations face disruptive business challenges, 86 percent of companies that value leadership development programs were able to respond more quickly to threats than organizations who did not prioritize this discipline.

Organizations equipped to handle turmoil invest in programs that focus development on asking the best questions, a trait most organizations lack. The Bersin Report by Deloitte found that only 30 percent of organizations rate their first-line leaders as highly capable, and less

Are we asking enough questions?

than half believe their midlevel leaders are highly capable.[103] Are we asking enough questions?

In a world drowning in opinions, have you asked enough questions today—of yourself, your team, or your business?

WHAT NOW?

When does your lack of questioning show up? What does it cost you, and what one thing can you practice today to invite others to question you?

"It is better to debate a question without settling it
than to settle a question without debating it."

JOSEPH JOUBERT

SIMPLIFY EVERYTHING

"Wise is the one who learns to dumb it down."

CURTIS TYRONE JONES

Why do most presentations lack a straightforward, uncomplicated, synthesized story? Ironically, the people who struggle the most to convey a narrative clearly are the ones with the most access to information, such as analysts, creatives, and researchers. This year I sat through a dozen senior-level executive meetings, and most of them lacked vision, structure, and inspiration. The presentations become littered with too many charts, unconnected ideas, and irrelevancy. The lack of a cohesive through line in the presentations caused boredom and disinterest for most of the audience members, but it wasn't their fault. The brain is lazy, and irrelevant material causes us to look for shortcuts or even shut down altogether. Too often, presentations repel the viewer when they should be a compelling accent to the story you're trying to tell. Let's face it, we all get bored when the content is not energizing.

Where presentations go wrong

I was recently sharing with a team that only one in twenty people remembers statistics after a presentation, yet over half remember a cohesive story.[104] With almost three quarters of the buying experience being determined by how the customer feels they are being treated,[105] the facts take a back seat and only matter when they build on an idea or uncover a deeper truth.

Psychologist Glenn Wilson found that the prefrontal cortex, which helps us prioritize tasks, is easily distracted when presented with new information or too many priorities.[106] Confusing or overwhelming amounts of information cause our IQ to fall by as much as ten points. Paradoxically, too many charts make everyone in the room less smart. We must learn to radically simplify our discussions and get to the point more quickly.

Being succinct isn't just the antidote to dumbed-down conversations; it's the answer. Studies show that we listen at a rate three times faster than most people speak. When we are too wordy and repeat ourselves too often, we distract others from the larger story.

> **Being succinct isn't just the antidote to dumbed-down conversations; it's the answer.**

On average, we spend 60 percent of our conversations talking about ourselves rather than encouraging deeper discussions.[107] Too much unnecessary dialogue damages a good story, distracting our audience and causing frustration. What makes a difference?

Excessive dialogue plagues most of us, but the most effective influencers develop communication intuition. When they sense they are talking too much, they reassess the needs of the group. They immerse themselves in empathy and listen to what is said and not said, creating genuine encounters with others.

While we have slowly evolved from "How can I be convincing?" to "How can I be understood?" the best presentations are more than that. They are moments to facilitate higher-level conversations and discovery. And once your ego has left the room, you will be shocked by what you can learn from your audience. The real question is to ask, "What am I hearing?"

When we present ideas, we may get long winded, and our audiences' minds may wander. We must be smarter with how we structure business meetings and presentations. Like any conversation, after ninety seconds, it's time to ask a question or pause, allowing the discussion to breathe. If presentations are truly a "one-on-one" game, the rules demand that the other person gets the ball. Practice applying the ninety-second rule, start listening, and simply everything.

WHAT NOW?

When does your excessive nature show up? What does it cost you, and what one thing can you practice today to truly simplify complexity in your life?

"Sometimes our stop-doing list needs to be bigger than our to-do list."

PATTI DIGH

A PUBLIC SPEAKING SECRET

"You must learn to inhabit your song."

BRUCE SPRINGSTEEN

I am often anxious before any type of public talk. I can't concentrate on anything else, and I become edgy about nonessential details that could inhibit my preparation. Paradoxically, I'm thankful that I still experience this sense of insecurity because it's a gift that allows me to never take a moment for granted. Being on the edge is the lifeblood of staying present with the audience. It encourages you to prioritize relational connections in lieu of self-adulation.

Public presentations are nerve-racking—at times, even scary. What's the biggest public speaking mistake most people make? To quote Bruce Springsteen, "You must learn to inhabit your song."[108] When you inhabit your message, you become believable. Springsteen reminds us of a truth: the best artists (and speakers) become their message. They personify and are one with their song!

Before you prepare a presentation, think through your objective or how you'll address an audience. Take the time to assess if you and your communication are one. An audience must feel that the talk was designed specifically for them and that your message is one with them.

"You know it's a great song when others think it was written for them." —Bruce Springsteen

The most engaging communicators don't give just a presentation; they share compelling stories that connect with the listener on a personal level. They speak in plain language that encourages connection. The very best speakers are deeply aware of how they affect others, and they are experiential.

We think in visuals and stories and are compelled by images. In fact, we process images sixty thousand times faster than words![109] That is how we think. Bullet points are for shopping lists, not experiential presentations. Take the time to personally design slides that create emotion and imagery, not boredom.

The very best presenters and public speakers understand that a thirty-minute talk deserves fifteen hours of preparation. Crafting a winning story takes reflection, practice, eliciting others' opinions, and days of pondering.

Bullet points are for shopping lists, not experiential presentations.

What are your public speaking vulnerabilities?

We all have the same internal dialogue and script that runs in our head. And this script can serve us. You should be worried if you're not nervous. The best speakers embrace anxiety. Fear serves them. It means you are now ready to passionately share from the heart. It's an energy that needs to be harnessed.

When are you at your best? And what strategies help you become one with the audience? I have three ideas that work for me. Ask yourself:

- What makes you most *relaxed* during the first thirty seconds of a talk?

- Who in the room must you *personally connect* with prior to a talk?

- How can you *close* your talk in a way that allows the audience to know you personally?

These principles allow you to rise above the anxiety and tap into your best, while keeping everything in a healthy perspective. Here is one last idea worth considering: kill the techniques.

There is nothing more annoying than watching a speaker try to earn the heart of an audience through praise, jokes, and an inauthentic emotional story that creates false intimacy. Learn to share parts of your own story. The only rule that governs a good talk is to share ideas that you are passionate about, with your own voice, while connecting and serving the audience. That's it!

We all fight the impulse to copy another's style. There is nothing wrong with modeling others, but the only sustainable approach is to learn to embrace your own voice and flaws. Practice becoming one with your message and the *moment*.

WHAT NOW?

When does your lack of preparation show up? What does it cost you, and what one thing can you practice today to be one with your audience?

"It usually takes me more than three weeks to prepare a good impromptu speech."

MARK TWAIN

MASTER IMPROVISATION

"The strangest thing you can do on stage is to think about what you're doing."

PETER WOLF

University of Michigan enthusiasts call their school the "Harvard of the West" because of a long-forgotten Ivy League quota restriction that funneled the East Coast's best students westward. But a more apt comparison to the merit of Harvard is the legendary comic factory Second City, which waggishly says, "Harvard is the Second City of higher education." When it comes to talent development in improvisational comedy, there is no one better. John Candy, John Belushi, Bill Murray, Chris Farley, Eugene Levy, Catherine O'Hara, Martin Short, Tina Fey, Dan Aykroyd, and Stephen Colbert are just a few of the icons to refine their craft of improvisation at Second City. Few places have generated a pattern of success comparable to Second City, and virtually none have fostered their culture of excellence.

The arts have much to teach us about communication, presence, and impact than most business development seminars ever could. And Second City is the exalted one of impromptu skills, extemporaneous communication, and creativity. Second City executives Kelly Leonard and Tom Yorton's book, *Yes, And*, reveals improvisational techniques that can help any organization develop innovators, encourage adaptable leaders, and build transformational businesses.[110] Are you comfortable building your improvisational skills through the eyes of a comic?

YES, AND

An open, nonjudgmental culture is where the best comedy is birthed and where invention is found. Second City refers to this as a "Yes, and" mindset. The artists practice building off each other's energy, ideas, and awareness and affirming each other's unique talent through requiring performers to start and reply to every sentence with "Yes, and ..."

The paradox of this transitional phrase is that it seems limiting but is completely liberating. Teams that embrace "Yes, and" are more inventive, quicker to solve problems, and create stronger engagement.

THE TEAM, THE TEAM, THE TEAM

In improvisational theatre, a breakthrough artist becomes a star because of, not despite, relationships with their peers. They practice cocreating with the audience and embrace failure as the ultimate teacher.

This may be the single greatest learning from Second City: as soon as the "Failure isn't an option" mentality is replaced with "Failure must be an option," every missed joke becomes a moment for brilliant self-degrading humor, and the team is able to work without fear of error. You are part of an ecosystem, and your personal success is contingent on helping your partner thrive. There is no place for lone wolves on this stage. You win or lose as a creative troop.

FOLLOW THE FOLLOWER

Leadership is dynamic: it's about discovering and utilizing talent, not protecting your status. Second City utilizes a "Follow the follower" model of improvisation. They teach the idea that power and status shifts within members of the group depending on the topic at hand. During a skit, it is often unclear which member is leading the scene as the performers are fluid. When leadership is required, the colleague with the appropriate idea or skill assumes leadership in that moment.

Leadership is dynamic: it's about discovering and utilizing talent, not protecting your status.

Too often sales, marketing, and business leaders appear rigid and leave the impression of working off a script. A senior retail buyer once shared with me, "Way too many people who call on me are flying blind to my needs, motives, and how I do business. They walk in here, and the first thing they do is tell me about themselves. They failed to immediately connect with me."

Most people believe they are good listeners. As the authors lay out, "There is a big difference between listening and understanding." When things get hectic, the real listening begins—and it's not undermined by status or title. When you establish real trust with another, you have permission to be ruthlessly candid and to lead when necessary. That is true authenticity and relationship. How do we practice the improvisational model? Can you give over control to others? When one is improvising, their eyes are not on themselves; they are focused outward. They are present.

WHAT NOW?

When does your lack of flexibility show up? What does it cost you, and what one thing can you practice today to epitomize the "Yes, and" mentality?

"The strength of the team is each individual member. The strength of each member is the team."

PHIL JACKSON

THE FIRST SIXTY SECONDS

"Every time I look in the mirror /
 All these lines on my face getting clearer."

AEROSMITH

Iconic music begins with an opening that you can't forget. The lyrics are emotional, engaging, and personal. It pulls the listener in, inviting them to go on a journey hand in hand with the artist. Similarly, from a young age, we learn that the opening sentence of a story or play is the "hook" that reels the audience in and invites them to the table.

That first line matters, and in the case of music, it gives the artist permission to move forward with the rest of the song. Like a song, the first line of a presentation paints a picture; it sets the atmosphere and allows you the confidence to continue. The first minute creates momentum for the rest of your story. Consider your last discussion: Did the opening give you permission to move forward, or did you lose the audience immediately?

Researchers believe that first impressions are created in under three seconds.[111] In the blink of an eye, people assess your competence, aggressiveness, intelligence, and trustworthiness. As you finish your first line, you've already been sized up and judged by audience members. Observers automatically and unconsciously conduct a mental shortcut, assessing whether they like or dislike, trust, or mistrust.

Daniel Kahneman, psychologist, Nobel laureate, and author of *Thinking, Fast And Slow,* has found that most people can predict accurately whether they will like a person, but they are also often wrong.[112] The brain doesn't like ambiguity; it would rather make quick, clean decisions devoid of nuance.

Kahneman's research shows that our expectations tend to be self-fulfilling. One's beliefs and assumptions of another person will directly influence the traits they choose to observe. This is called confirmation bias, the tendency to search for and favor information that confirms our own preexisting beliefs, and we're all susceptible to it.

> **One's beliefs and assumptions of another person will directly influence the traits they choose to observe.**

A few years ago, Microsoft uncovered that the average attention span has fallen 33 percent, from twelve to eight seconds.[113] We now live in a world where "capturing one's attention" is an invaluable art form. Most people are still stuck in "PowerPoint thinking," a regimented and overblown approach to communication. But the best communicators are true, concise, and flexible. Are you able to get to the point and hold another's attention? The research proves you may not be as good as you think. On average, people spend 60 percent of conversations talking about themselves.[114] Those people are lost at sea and don't even know it. I have discovered three big communication traps:

THE THREE TRAPS

EMBELLISHMENT. Brilliant writers share one thing: extreme editing. They unapologetically and mercilessly cut any unnecessary elements. Communications must remain minimal, clear, and thoughtful. While most of us aren't routinely exposed to merciless editors, if you ever get to see their process, you'll realize there is *always* an opportunity to cut. Trim the fat from your discussions—learn brevity.

UNREADINESS. You want to be irrelevant? Don't prepare properly. "Under promising and overperforming" is the most proven, yet least practiced, adage today. There is nothing worse than someone who shows up for a discussion and doesn't understand your needs, agenda, or communication preference. The best communicators think like surgeons, diagnosing the situation and context before they prescribe a solution.

ISOLATION. Stretching is inherently uncomfortable. To be present and receptive in a room full of people is an incredibly difficult feat. The best communicators are in the moment with you, adapting their communication style to be congruent with yours, whether you're alone or with a team. It's not about "them," it's about "you." In a word, they are highly "present."

Mark Twain shared, "It usually takes me more than three weeks to prepare an impromptu speech."[115] The best presentations (or discussions) have no fluff. They have been edited down to the essence of the message. Keep the tangents at the dinner table with old friends. Anyone can give a thirty-slide presentation; very few can share an idea with precision, in one slide. The more concise the presentation, the more time necessary to create it.

- Is your communication simple, clear, direct, conversational, and relatable?

- Can you grab someone's attention and still make your point in less than sixty seconds?

In a Customer Centric Selling blog, John Holland shares, "Filler words are verbal crutches and can be distracting. Don't talk just to fill up space! Pause, listen, don't make noise."[116]

One must *create* a compelling sales story that is simple, experiential, and unique while capturing another's attention. Don't let needless details detract from your message, hindering the soul of your message.

Research reminds us that we only have a few seconds to pique a recipient's interest and make a bid for an attention extension! Why is it that most of the time we fumble away the moment or transition into a tired old pitch?

That is why the first sixty seconds of a meeting is so critical. You are being critiqued whether you like it or not. Here are three ideas to start a meeting:

1. Start a discussion with a direct question that uncovers or validates "unrecognized" challenges.

2. Convey a "what if" question, offering a vision of what could be cocreated and the gap it fills.

3. Demonstrate that you keenly understand their deepest challenges, and prove you can solve them.

People often talk too much, sound scripted, use too much jargon, and discuss irrelevant information. Their words are far from compelling and do not invite deeper engagement.

The very best have become one with their message, allowing them to stay in the moment. They are skilled at answering the question, "Why should you care about what I am sharing?"

WHAT NOW?

When does your lack of clarity show up? What does it cost you, and what one thing can you practice today to express more conciseness?

"I would have written you a shorter letter if I had more time."

BLAISE PASCAL

IT'S TIME TO GO DEEP

"Trust is a great force multiplier."

TOM RIDGE

I once received a phone call from an old friend who emphatically presented the merits of collaborating with him on a project his company was spearheading within our industry. For twenty minutes, he presented a binder full of reasons why it would (in his opinion) be good for me to invest my time, energy, and creativity in his initiative. After he laid out the pitch, I asked him a simple question, "Would you like to better understand my thoughts?" My old friend paused and replied, "Ummmm, sure, that would be a good idea, Dan. Tell me what you are trying to accomplish these days." We both started laughing, and I proceeded to share how my coaching business had evolved since we last spoke.

Most sales leaders do not invest enough time understanding the stated and unstated agenda of their customers, partners, and teammates. They rarely uncover hidden problems or stress points that need to be solved. My friend forgot the golden rule of sales: *it's not about **you**; it's about **us***. A customer meeting emphasizes diagnosing the situation long before prescribing a solution.

THE SECRET

Elevating a relationship isn't something you do; it's the result of everything you've done. Most people aren't looking for highly differentiated solutions; they are looking for reliability, results, and trust. Yet too often we spend time in transactional discussions versus forging higher-level partnerships. What are the secrets of higher-level trusting relationships?

They start with appreciating patience and not forcing premature or unnatural conversations. People embrace relationships with someone they know, like, trust, need, want, and value. If any of these three pillars are weakened, the relationship is vulnerable to collapse.

Heart-level relationships exist when both parties have a deeper understanding of the other's unstated interests. And this only occurs when the relationship is cemented in trust. I refer to this as the "Three Cornerstones of Trust." People who trust others believe three things:

- You care about my personal needs, not just your own interests.

- You authentically want to better understand me as a person.

- You are willing to connect me to other people or solutions to help me.

Business relationships, like any relationship, must be expansive and purposeful. Transactional relationships are not sustainable.

HOW DO WE ENCOURAGE HEALTHIER MEETINGS WITH OTHERS?

Stephen Colbert's music director and band leader, Jon Batiste, once stated: "A live performance is a collaboration with the audience; you ride the ebb and flow of the crowd's energy."[117] We must set the tone for peaceful, honest discussion. The audience creates an atmosphere for the artist to accelerate, ideate, and perform—knowing full well they are rewarded for doing so.

A top executive recently shared with me, "If you don't care about my agenda, I won't care about yours." The job of a sales or service agency is to uncover hidden problems, escalating costs, and risk of failing to implement a solution. Executives want partners who solve problems and think holistically about their business. Your best allies help you uncover and neutralize threats before they take root.

Recently, I shared with a client the algorithm of preparing for a very important customer meeting. Success is driven by ten preplanning questions.

THE DEEP DIVE

1. What are the customer's highest-level priorities and growth strategies?

2. What are the customer's competitive threats, risks, and pressure points?

3. What obstacles, problems, or constraints will you have to overcome to strengthen the relationship?

4. What additional knowledge, skills, resources, or capabilities will you require to achieve your strategic objectives with the customer?

5. Why is it necessary that the customer do what you propose? What is the proof?

6. What internal customer politics have you not fully appreciated and are hindering your story?

7. Which of your hidden assets could address the customer's pressure points?

8. Which influencers must you ensure attend the discussion, and what is their role in the meeting?

9. How can you neutralize your competitor's most unique strengths?

10. What one big idea could transform your customer relations?

HUMANIZE THE CONVERSATION

Customer development is less about selling and more about helping others with change management. Many of us get stuck in "pitch mode" and forget to humanize the conversation. Extensive measures are always taken to avoid a loss, and it's your job to tailor the conversation by helping others understand the risk of complacency. Necessity is the great paradigm shifter, not opportunities.

Comedian Jerry Seinfeld once said, "A joke must focus on the structure, word choice, syntax, pacing and rhythm. It's performance art. Comedians think in minutes."[118] I've found that an effective approach to a meaningful meeting or call follows similar tenets to what Seinfeld is describing. Often our pace can be too forward or domineering. We lose track of the rhythm and forget to let the conversation breathe. These conversational respites allow for freeform dialogue, uncovering previously unstated goals and agendas. The pause is where true gems in a conversation are unearthed.

When done well, big meetings are moments to strengthen relationships, problem solve, and better understand many of the unstated needs

It's not about you; it's about us.

of another. When maximized, they are moments when your preparation is so thorough that you are free to improvise in the moment. The algorithm of planning for a big customer meeting is rooted in thoughtfully diagnosing the unstated needs of the customer. *It's not about you; it's about us.*

WHAT NOW?

When does lack of alignment show up? What does it cost you, and what one thing can you practice today to understand others' unstated needs?

"Customer service is an attitude, not a department."

MO HARDY

REFLECTION TIME

QUESTIONS TO PONDER

1. We often overestimate the value we provide others; how do others experience you?

2. Have others in your sphere ever told you that you are guilty of intervening too often?

3. Do you have a secret need to position yourself as the smartest person in the room? And why is that?

4. As a leader you're contagious; what are others catching from you?

5. Each of us have a finite amount of energy; who or what steals your energy?

6. Are you known for conducting fierce, transparent conversations, or do you often shrink away?

7. Active listeners are participative, immersive, and assertive, assessing what's stated and unstated.

8. The best speakers become "one" with their message. How do you personalize your presentations?

9. Can you grab someone's attention and still make your point in less than sixty seconds?

10. Do you start meetings asking, "Why are we here, and what needs to get solved?"

ORGANIZATIONAL

Blind spots don't exclusively exist in personal and relational spaces; organizations must also guard against unhealthy behaviors and practices. Organizations that emphasize holistic, healthy, and likeable cultures are often rewarded with stronger customer engagement, employee retention, and loyalty.

When your company or team has no clear soul or purpose, it succumbs to wasted time and hidden agendas. It struggles to prioritize important issues, lacking cohesiveness in big moments. Organizations need to be able to cut through the noise of an industry and identify which elements in their game plan are responsible for majority of their success. They need extreme clarity into what makes them special and courage to walk away from activities and relationships that no longer serve them.

Organizations must be committed to building deeper and even more trusting relationships than ever before.

The rules of partnerships have changed. Consumers are making more thoughtful choices about everything, and organizations must be committed to building deeper and even more trusting relationships than ever before. Consumers have options when it comes to who gets their next dollar, and partnerships must be transparent and relational, and both parties must be mutually invested in each other's business.

Successful organizations create distinct products and invite consumer critique and input at every step in the development process. Cocreation is a necessity today, yet too often, companies still believe in a controlling, top-down philosophy whereby the "voice of the customer" is not included. When the customer is excluded from the creation process, valuable input is lost due to headstrong or fearful leadership. These organizations have lost their sense of collaboration or have lost the script altogether.

The top commercial organizations recognize that every internal department serves the consumer, and everyone on the team must think like small business owners. No one has the time or energy for internal politics, and every department must simplify processes, move quicker, and learn faster to help the commercial team meet the changing needs of the consumer and their partners.

Moving into the future, every organization will be confronted with new competitors and the incremental costs associated with operating in a volatile, uncertain, and ambiguous world. This section will challenge you and your teams to operate as "*one*," allowing everyone to team up seamlessly, courageously, and holistically with each other.

"Organizations and teams are ecosystems that demand water and sunlight. Healthy teams are nourished, fed, and protected. They are built on deliberate practice."

EMBRACING AN UNPREDICTABLE WORLD

"Despite all this rapid change in the computing industry,
we are still at the beginning of the digital revolution."

SATYA NADELLA

On the evening of March 20, 2020, I sat in my office deeply troubled, wondering if most of my clients would have the financial flexibility to participate in our annual leadership forum events, or engage in any coaching or training activities as the COVID pandemic started to reach a tipping point. That Friday evening, I had a very solemn conversation with my wife, Michele, sharing with her that there was a risk that everything I do would be perceived by our partners as nonessential. When panic kicks in, budgets are always dramatically cut, and coaching and training is the first to go. We planned for the worst, and over that weekend, I redesigned my whole business model. Almost two years later, I realize that moment forced me to reinvent my coaching, training, and consulting business through more of a digital and remote lens. The pandemic was the catalyst for transformation, but in retrospect, I should have acknowledged and embraced this technology much earlier, taking advantage of a more intimate form of communication.

Innovations in technology have created seismic shifts in myriad industries, offering both opportunity and destruction. We're all looking for certainty in this increasingly uncertain world, and we overprotect ourselves when faced with potential loss. This inherent response can lead us to make bad decisions in the face of risky situations. Psychologists Daniel Kahneman and Amos Tversky's Prospect Theory research validates this. The psychologists theorized that we often choose to embrace the comfortable route that is less valuable in lieu of something riskier yet more advantageous.[119] When are you most vulnerable to accepting comfortable answers, versus embracing the right answer?

SO HOW DO WE CONFIDENTLY NAVIGATE AN UNPREDICTABLE WORLD?

VUCA is an acronym developed in the wake of the Cold War to describe the complexities of a postwar world, and the principles of VUCA translate well to any situation where the world feels turbulent and erratic. We live in a culture of increasing volatility, uncertainty, complexity, and ambiguity (VUCA) today. The clients I work with face daily hypercompetition only made worse by an anxiety-ridden competitive environment. A substantial swath of the workforce is feeling the instability, with over one in three people reporting they consistently feel more anxious than they did a year ago.[120]

The sooner we get comfortable being unbalanced, the more versatile we become.

During coaching sessions, I encourage leaders to pause and recognize the blind spots, personal

196

behaviors, or lies that hinder their performance and enjoyment. Take a moment to quickly assess how competitive you are through the lens of VUCA:

- **VOLATILITY** – Are you broadly preparing for change and accurately forecasting potential threats?

- **UNCERTAINTY** – Are you investing in advisors and expanding your contextual knowledge?

- **COMPLEXITY** – Do you have diverse specialists in your corner who complement each other's strengths to face a wide array of problems?

- **AMBIGUITY** – Have you embraced a "test and learn" mindset to highlight next steps?

VUCA should create stress, but it is the catalyst for new growth. The sooner we get comfortable being unbalanced, the more versatile we become.

WE LOVE WHAT WE KNOW.

We tend to hold on to our most familiar ideas and relationships, even if there are better alternatives. NN, the European financial services company, discovered that we overweigh options that appear safe, even when they are not. The research showed that we normally invest in smaller "sure things" rather than investing in larger bets with dramatic upside.[121]

We close doors fearing a world that seems uncertain, unknown, and unsure. What unresolved discussions should you have with your team this week that push you out of your comfort zone?

WE ALSO LOVE WHAT IS SIMPLE.

Between three options, we normally choose the simplest. When multiple similar objects are present, people tend to choose the option that differs from the rest (the simplest), a bias known as the Isolation Effect. Our internal response is to distance ourselves from anything that creates discomfort or pain. For most of us, "complexity" equals "pain," and we instinctually run from it. We do this even when it is the wrong choice.

The VUCA paradigm shines a light on the inevitable: things will continue to change. Asking the above questions force us to objectively assess how we are handling the unavoidable unknown. We are guided by our subconscious, which detests volatility, uncertainty, complexity, and ambiguity.

Truth is rarely simple or certain. Are you playing tight or embracing a changing world?

WHAT NOW?

When do volatility, uncertainty, complexity, and ambiguity knock you off your game? What does it cost you, and what one thing can you practice today to dance with VUCA?

"Tactics is knowing what to do when there
is something to do; strategy is knowing
what to do when there is nothing to do."

SAVIELLY TARTAKOWER

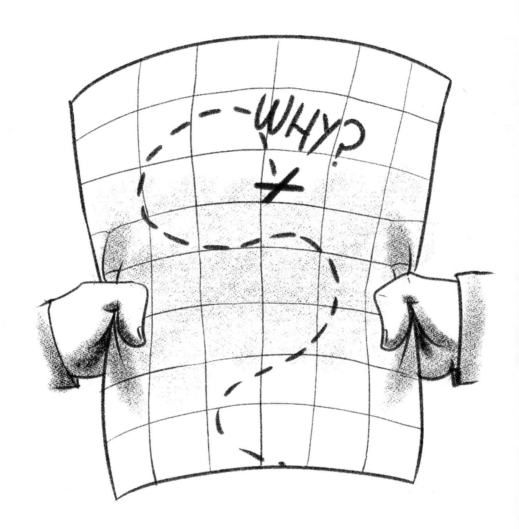

WHAT IS YOUR WHY?

"Cooperation is the thorough conviction that nobody
can get there unless everybody gets there."

VIRGINIA BURDEN

In 1979, the San Francisco 49ers won only two games. Within two years, legendary coach Bill Walsh had transformed the team into a Super Bowl–winning organization and ushered in a decade of success. Walsh attributes his success to the culture that he carefully tended during his tenure: "It was a way of doing things, a leadership philosophy, that has as much to do with core values, principles, and ideals, as with blocking, tackling, and passing."[122] When culture is right, the foundation is right, and we are in a better position to create success. Are there any cracks in your foundation?

While most companies tout their values publicly, most are often shrouded in inconsistencies. They are promises often unkept, aspirations never fully realized, and can sometimes be the antithesis of an organization's reality. Where there should be guiding inspiration, there is a breach of contract. The healthiest companies and leaders know that the answer to your "Why?" is integral to building loyalty and purpose within the company's ranks and within your target consumer base.

Research shows that 55 percent of Fortune 100 companies say "integrity" is a core value, 49 percent espouse customer satisfaction, and 40 percent value teamwork.[123] While these are all great qualities, they are hardly differentiators and do not speak to a deeper sense of purpose. The "why" is much deeper than a word on a wall. It's the heart of your story and the through line of your organization.

There is perhaps no greater representation of this concept than the clothing manufacturer Patagonia. Its founder, Yvon Chouinard, has been the gold standard of walking in purpose since the company's founding in the 1970s, and the organization continues to zealously iterate on ways it can champion sustainability and conservation. From experiential initiatives such as company-wide tours of harmful conventional cotton fields, to 100 percent donation of its Black Friday sales to grassroots environmental nonprofits, Patagonia has never faltered in its stalwart commitment to saving the planet. Chouinard poetically reminds us in his book, *Let My People Go Surfing*, "How you climb a mountain is more important than reaching the top."[124] He recognizes the reality that being the biggest or selling the most merchandise is a hollow and unsustainable model devoid of purpose and longevity. The "how" matters and so does the "why."

A great business strategy will always falter in the long run without passion and purpose. If you don't have a big enough "why" fueling your culture, you are vulnerable. IBM ex-CEO Lou Gerstner asserts, "Corporate culture is not part of the game: It is the game."[125] The heart of a great culture is a compelling "why."

> **A great business strategy will always falter in the long run without passion and purpose.**

Having direct conversations with friends or advisors to rectify aspects of your leadership style that may be hindering you takes real courage. Friends will call out your best and often fearlessly tell you the truth about your flaws. If you want to get to your "why," you need to understand how you are showing up with others.

Here are three questions worth exploring at your next team meeting.

1. What is your team's "why," and does it compel others to unify as a team?

2. What's your personal leadership story, and does it inspire and encourage others to share theirs?

3. How do you affect others, and do you bring out the best in your team?

A sculptor chips away at stone to uncover the creation within. Likewise, one's mission is often buried within, waiting to be discovered. Healthy leaders do not run from these three questions; they embrace them with fervor.

WHAT NOW?

When does your lack of purpose show up? What does it cost you, and what one thing can you practice today to solidify your personal purpose statement?

"You do not merely want to be considered just the best of the best. You want to be considered the only one who does what you do."

JERRY GARCIA

THE ART OF FACILITATION

"Curiosity has its own reason for existence."

ALBERT EINSTEIN

Recently, I was working with a contractor on some changes we were making in our home. I was struggling to work with him because the conversation felt very one sided. He was a wealth of technological information, but my needs felt entirely unheard. One-way conversations filled with too many words, limited nuance, and narrow self-awareness can be one of the most draining and unproductive uses of our time. When we share ideas or opinions with great certainty, it often doesn't land well. We get lost in the exhilaration of presentation and fail to embrace the "art of facilitation." How do you experience others who exhibit too much certainty and fail to bring you into the conversation?

Are you occasionally guilty of excessive presentation and not enough facilitation?

Most organizations love to "present" their ideas, but the highest performing companies embrace a different set of skills: questions, strategic reflection, and the ability to moderate a curious discussion. When you ignore open dialogue, you miss crucial discussion and constructive opposition. Are you occasionally guilty of excessive presentation and not enough facilitation?

Just as a conductor keeps an orchestra in sync, a facilitator keeps the discussion on task. These facilitators can identify which streams of the discussion are fruitful and which are distracting, leading to broader dialogue and mutual ownership of the meeting's outcome. They reframe problems and encourage teammates to stay open minded so they can creatively problem solve and effectively think through options. Facilitation skills are rare, and they are vital to tapping into the varying ideas of diverse teams.

A gifted facilitator pays attention to group cohesion and relational dynamics while staying unbiased as a conversation ebbs and flows. The best stays neutral as they ride the discussion wave with teammates while still giving merit to each point of view. Meeting participants focus on discussion content while the facilitator monitors the process, energy, and openness in the room.

THE THREE STEPS OF MEETING FACILITATON

Like a great coach, facilitators are nondirective and assist others through the creative process. They draw out opinions and uncover challenges without taking the spotlight away from participants. The best senior leaders are facilitators, structuring their meeting to encourage all members of the team to participate evenly and candidly. In my research I have noted three steps to effectively facilitate a team or customer meeting.

STEP 1: RULES OF ENGAGEMENT

Delineate your expectations early and clearly. Prior to a meeting, define the rules of engagement, expected outcomes, and discussion norms. It is important to let discussions breathe and develop naturally, but gaining agreement on a simple meeting structure such as prearranged roles and time allocation can enrich the conversation. Share the expectations for how conflict and rambling discussion will be handled. Moreover, it is always smart to highlight the importance of listening, candor, and respect for dissenting viewpoints. You must frame how the meeting will "feel" prior to starting the discussion.

STEP 2: EMBRACE NEUTRALITY

A facilitator is a conversation catalyst and should not manipulate or lead the exchange toward a predetermined destination. An adept moderator establishes a firm yet flexible framework that directs the flow of conversation without letting too many personal beliefs taint the debate.

The best facilitators are tuned into the relational dynamics of attendees and subtly soften the politics in the room. Their instincts and nonthreatening communication skills allow them the freedom to ask difficult questions without associates feeling like they are being led down a preordained path. They utilize thoughtful questions to assess group commitment, reframe challenges, and formulate areas of agreement. They are in a trusting relationship and working "for" everyone in the room.

STEP 3: CREATE AN ATMOSPHERE

Managing relational conflict and courageous discussions is part of all relationships. Without a tempered voice to mediate conflict, discussions can quickly become counterproductive or downright harmful. When you combine multiple interests and diverse personalities in a room, conflict is common, the trick is to channel that friction in a positive direction. Facilitators must create an atmosphere that is safe, open, and creative, even when the heat goes up. Since individuals rarely share their hidden motives, facilitators must exhibit dexterity, uncovering deeper needs while also forging an atmosphere that is secure and protected.

The best meetings practice radical transparency and healthy dissent while protecting relationships and solving big problems.

WHAT NOW?

When does your lack of cooperation show up? What does it cost you, and what one thing can you practice today to facilitate open discussions with others?

"It is not the answer that
enlightens, but the question."

EUGENE IONESCO

DRUCKER IS STILL RIGHT— HOW TO BE DISTINCT!

"A goal without a plan is just a wish."

ANTOINE DE SAINT-EXUPERY

I often wonder how many failed start-ups would entirely reinvent their inception if they had taken the following question more seriously: "Is your business that different from your competitors?" A good friend of mine started a data management business and for five years suffered through financial challenges, marital strife, and overwhelming psychological strain. He thought he understood the market, his consumer, and how to manage limited cash flow. In retrospect, he misjudged most facets of his operation and closed his doors frustrated, broke, and reeling. Most businesses and leaders are not as distinct as they think they are. When have you recently underestimated your competition, or overestimated your advantage?

There are over 28 million businesses in the US alone. Big and small, all aspire to succeed, yet most fail. According to Bloomberg, 80 percent of entrepreneurs who start businesses fail within the first eighteen months.[126]

Most businesses and leaders are not as distinct as they think they are.

Most new businesses are not unique, and they overestimate their point of difference and underestimate their competitors. They miss the mark because they do not understand their customers and have an inability to convey a coherent message.

Peter Drucker, the father of modern management, author of thirty-nine books, and creator of much of our business vocabulary, provided the map to be distinct. He came up with five questions that cut through the noise, and they remain just as relevant to business today.

DRUCKER'S FIVE QUESTIONS:[127]

WHAT IS YOUR MISSION?

Establishing a succinct and simple mission creates a sense of purpose within the company's ranks, allowing the team to consciously work toward a long-term objective. A truly compelling mission creates cohesion, emotion, and inspiration. It holds the team together when the going gets tough.

WHO IS YOUR CUSTOMER?

Most companies throw a wide net and try to fish for any customer who bites. This is dated, inefficient and dangerous. The smartest organizations draw a line in the sand, inviting anyone who unites with their mission to come join the family. If properly identified, these people are the heart of your business and assist you in the development of the next iteration of products and services. Take pride in knowing not everyone should be your customer.

WHAT DOES THE CUSTOMER VALUE?

Consumers purchase products, but they value experiences. Determining what is truly meaningful to the customer is often deeper than words; it is a feeling. Consumers will commit to a relationship with a brand only when their deepest values are being met. Customers will only enter authentic, emotional relationships with brands they trust.

WHAT ARE YOUR RESULTS?

Uncover three to five trends everyone on the team should be thinking about and monitoring that will help you achieve your mission. Most organizations track and scorecard too many irrelevant measurements, straying from the core tenet of successful organizations: to satisfy the most important needs of your consumer and advance your mission.

WHAT IS YOUR PLAN?

The most relevant plans are crystal clear and flexible, based on changing dynamics and new data. Structure within your planning process is still vital, but the rate at which change occurs now demands that plans be agile, fluid, and modifiable. If you have set aspirational goals, listened to the critique of customers and employees, and commit to cocreation with others, your plan of attack is well on its way.

No matter how successful a company gets, continually asking these questions remains vital; even Drucker never stopped asking these questions. Mastering these five questions creates a blueprint to help your company uncover its true personality, potential, and purpose.

Drucker stated, "Leadership should not even try to guess the answers but should always go to the customers in a systematic quest for those answers." His philosophy requires persistent vulnerability and self-critique. It is a commitment to nurture and retain what is working, while discarding habits that do not stir growth. Drucker's blueprint prevents bad habits from festering and provides a glue between management, employees, and customers.

As author Peter Economy said, "The answers you get (from Drucker's questions) will provide you with the clear roadmap you need to build a highly effective—and profitable—venture."[128] Even more than that, it is a tool to cut the noise from your decision-making process.

In moments of struggle, always return to the five questions.

WHAT NOW?

When does your lack of planning show up? What does it cost you, and what one thing can you practice today to start creating a blueprint that clearly defines your goals?

"Simplicity is the ultimate sophistication. "

LEONARDO DA VINCI

ARE YOU A COURAGEOUS COACH?

"The unexamined life is not worth living."

SOCRATES

One of the leaders I have coached for years recently shared with me, "Our business is draining my soul, and I have lost my mojo." He went on to explain how he was not confronting difficult behaviors with his associates, nor did he have the patience to coach some of his more difficult teammates. He was no longer having fun, and everyone was experiencing his lack of energy. Consequently, many people distanced themselves from him, not wanting to trigger frustration or disappointment. Most people are looking for leaders who continue to do the "inner work" on themselves, creating healthy, transparent, and courageous coaching cultures. They are looking for thoughtful, inspired, and courageous coaches.

In 1950, it took fifty years for medical knowledge to double. It is now believed to be every seventy-three days.[129] The speed and magnitude of change in institutional knowledge can create insecurity and instability. In my own executive share groups, eight of ten leaders are feeling more uneasy, restless, and apprehensive than they did three years ago. Additionally, according to Gallup, nearly 85 percent of employees worldwide are not engaged or are actively disengaged at work, despite companies throwing more resources at this opportunity than ever before.[130] Team leaders have a choice: practice being a courageous coach or risk losing your team.

Are you burning too much energy managing internal politics, coping with passive-aggressive associates, or constantly fighting "know-it-alls" within your organization? If so, your team, and coaching acumen must evolve. The future is "energy management," not "time management." Team cohesion is a consistent prerequisite for creating an environment where your energy is maximized. Energy is a finite, invaluable currency to be protected or carefully allocated.

In holistic cultures colleagues adopt an open-book mentality to feedback at every level within the organization. Associates coach their bosses, teammates vertically share feedback with their peers, and senior leaders have the freedom to candidly share their unfiltered thoughts downstream with everyone on the team. How do we build holistic, healthy cultures and courageously coach in a transforming world?

The best coaches are not heavy handed in their counsel. They're Socratic, facilitative, and nondirective. Coaches are the catalysts of heightened capacity, confidence, and resilience. They assist others in identifying personal goals and uncovering roadblocks that are hindering the realization of those goals. Their commitment expands the self-awareness of others and builds healthy pipelines of communication.

THE PILLARS OF COURAGEOUS COACHING:

1. **STORY:** To be an effective coach, you must understand your team's personal story. The fears, triggers, and past experiences of the group influence their mindset and relationships today. Our past story shapes everything and everyone we touch today.

2. **EXPECTATIONS:** As a coach, you must be crystal clear on what the individual is trying to achieve and appreciate the inner roadblocks hindering their momentum. Expectation setting is essential for the long-term health of most relationships, and a coaching relationship is no different. Allow the associate to outline their personal definition of success and try to refrain from overassumption.

3. **TEAM DYNAMICS:** Every coaching discussion is a customized cocreation experience, expanding the emotional bandwidth and capacity of each other. The coach's role is to create a safe environment for the associate to honestly self-assess their mindset, game plan, and various roadblocks hindering progress. The associate owns the plan and must remain honest, open, and committed to collaborating with the coach on the mental preparation necessary to achieve their outcomes.

Courageous and fearless coaches help you confront the lies you tell yourself and assist you in calibrating the right steps to build positive momentum. Tomorrow's leaders understand that fearless discussion with emotionally transparent teams is essential in building a healthy, holistic organization.

WHAT NOW?

When does your lack of coaching courage show up? What does it cost you, and what one thing can you practice today to demonstrate fearless and thoughtful coaching?

"It's what you learn, after you know it all, that counts."

JOHN WOODEN

"WHOLE BRAIN" LEADERSHIP

"Management is doing things right; leadership is
doing the right things."

PETER DRUCKER

I love *The West Wing*, NBC's political drama television series created by Aaron Sorkin, which aired from 1999 to 2006. I have watched the series twice, and the writing, acting, and storytelling never disappoint. The series covers the tenure of Democratic president Josiah Bartlett, played by Martin Sheen. Sorkin was the lead writer during the foundational first four years of the series and creates a gestalt that carries throughout all eight years. *The West Wing*'s emotional and intellectual heft pulls you in, which is why the series has been ranked among the best television shows of all time by *Rolling Stone*, the *New York Daily News*, and The Writers Guild of America. The blend of head and heart is difficult to beat.

Here is my only rub on *The West Wing*. Sorkin's characters all rhetorically speak with a similar tone, tenure, pace, and feel. Almost every core character, of high or low profile, speak at a rapid rate, and most conversations include some form of personal banter and verbal jousting. Everyone sounds the same, carries a similar worldview, and tells the same type jokes. It is a fun reminder that even in the best fictious administrations (or organizations), we need diverse thinking, acting, and sounding members of the team. We need a complementary thinking (and sounding) team that comprises a whole brain.

We all have a preferred way of processing information and thinking through difficult problems. Research has shown that there are four primary modes of processing information. We sort information analytically, sequentially, interpersonally, or imaginatively. Most people, 90 percent, utilize multiple modes. Only 7 percent of people studied strongly prefer one mode over the others, and less than 3 percent are whole brained in their preferences, preferring all four quadrants equally.

Whole Brain® Thinking is a model designed by creativity researcher Ned Herrmann. The model shines a light on how we all process information differently. Herrmann used this as a metaphor for describing the four decision-making modes, pointing out that different activities require different mental processes. He discovered that these four thinking modes are essential to creating a holistic team.[131]

- **ANALYTICAL** – emphasizes facts, logic, and reasoning.

- **SEQUENTIAL** – emphasizes directions, details, planning, and step-by-step problem-solving.

- **INTERPERSONAL** – emphasizes listening, feelings, conveying ideas and collaboration.

- **IMAGINATIVE** – emphasizes bigger-picture thinking, challenging norms, creativity, and vision.

As leaders grow in power, their self-awareness decreases. Research shows that only 10–15 percent of people have high self-awareness. Self-awareness is an amalgamation of two skills: managing one's own state of mind while understanding how you affect others. Very few people are adept at both skills, and even fewer are aware of their own decision-making preferences and those of their team.

In hypercompetitive climates, organizations must embrace Whole Brain® Thinking. Change management expert John Kotter reminds us: "Individuals who keep large, complex organizations operating reliably and efficiently are managers. This is not what a leader does. A leader is visionary and empowers others while getting their emotional commitment."[132] A leader connects dots in a dynamic world, constructing purpose and harnessing talent while creating the culture. Kotter believes that "too many firms are over-managed and under-led" in a world of limited competitive advantage.

> **A leader connects dots in a dynamic world, constructing purpose and harnessing talent while creating the culture.**

Harvard's Rosabeth Moss Kanter flips the debate by stating that "strategy is never excellent on its own; the game is won on the playing field." She continues: "When a strategy looks brilliant, it's because of the quality of execution."[133]

The highest-performing organizations incorporate a unique blend of both leadership and execution skills. Leadership expert Bill George has shared many times that today we are seeing a different kind of organization: far less hierarchical with more collaboration, empowerment, and a global outlook. They have acquired a medley of distinct technical skills and "soft skills," to include adaptability, resilience, and emotional connection.[134] The future of teams is a fusion of logical, resourceful, collaborative, and creative people. The future is whole brain organizations.

WHAT NOW?

When does your lack of holistic thinking show up? What does it cost you, and what one thing can you practice today to engage others with your whole brain?

"There is nothing so useless as doing efficiently that which should not be done at all."

PETER DRUCKER

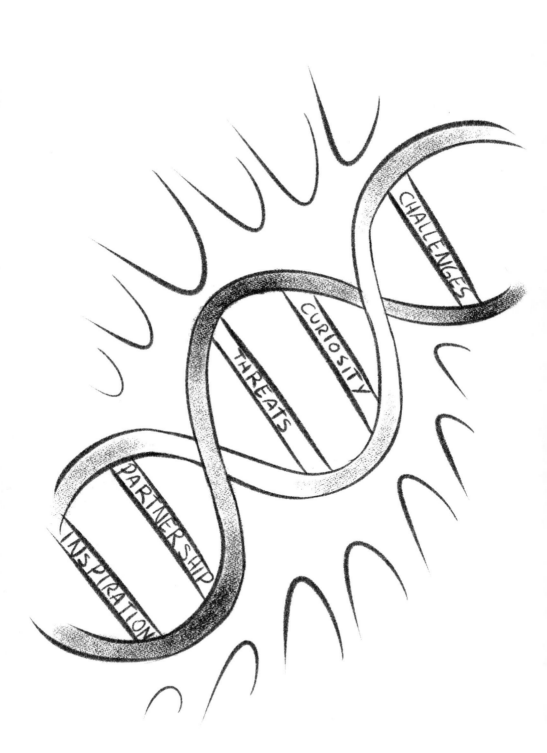

THE DNA OF ELITE TEAMS

"If the problems you have this year are the same problems you had last year, then you are not a leader. You are rather a problem on your own that must be solved."

ISRAELMORE AYIVOR

We always look for scapegoats.

TJ ran a little company that marketed specialty soaps and lotions for many of the top drug stores and high-end grocery outlets on the West Coast. It was a family-owned company that was a real success story. His father helped him get it off the ground, and TJ did the rest. He personally sold the initial products into a few retailers, and expanded his brands and presence year after year, partnering with most of the top retailers in the US. He managed every part of the operation, and he carried the financial, physical, and emotional burden for years. It cost him his first marriage, and like many entrepreneurs, his company defined him.

After twenty-five years of sales growth, he hit a wall, both personally and financially. What do you do when you are defined by something, and you become stagnant? If you are not healthy, you often blame others, never honestly considering that you could be the problem. TJ had not built an elite team, nor did he allow the talent he had attracted to utilize their talents. He did not understand that the role of a senior leader is to attract talent, understand their unique skills, and create an atmosphere for them to thrive. TJ could not allow his team to lead their job functions, because he could not let go. And it cost him much more than sales growth. It eventually cost him his company and his impact as a leader.

Gallup's latest State of the American Workplace research is essential reading for leaders looking to build and retain elite organizations. The research reports widespread disappointment in leadership, with eight in ten employees believing their boss lacks vision or clear communication.[135] Most teams are not in alignment and struggle from many dysfunctional behaviors. High-performing teams set an extremely high bar. Elite performance is scarce, estimated at 3–5 percent of any competitive segment. What's their secret?

The best general managers understand that having the most talent doesn't necessarily mean you have the best team. Elite teams are ecosystems where the sum is much bigger than the individual parts. Learning, and effectively distilling those learnings, is the growth engine. Jack Welch understood this: "An organization's ability to learn, and translate that learning into action rapidly, is the ultimate competitive advantage." A diverse, open, and emotionally healthy team is your competitive advantage.

ARE YOU CREATING A TEAM THAT EMBRACES THE "HOW"?

Almost six of ten senior executives believe their teams are underperforming, citing both lack of accountability and lack of communication as key culprits.[136] Building an elite team goes far beyond accumulating talent. On average, the highest-performing teams take five years of deliberate daily practice to attain elite status. They are a blend of talent and organizational fit, operating as one. How does an organization create a culture that has the potential to birth a great team?

In a podcast with John Eades, Sam Walker, author of *The Captain Class*, said: "The best leaders are always communicating, almost to the point where it's tiring. All of the captains of the greatest sports teams of all time were extremely effective communicators even though they weren't always eloquent."[137] In fact, the act of relentless communication and insight sharing is a huge part of a team's long-term success.

Alex Pentland shared in a *Harvard Business Review* article titled "The New Science of Building Great Teams" that high-performing teams possess an energy, creativity, and shared commitment that far surpasses other teams. The key to top performers lies not in the content of a team's discussions but in the style in which they communicated. It was discovered that a team's "patterns of communication (were the) most important predictor of a team's success."[138] The findings continue to say that those communication styles "are as significant as all the other factors—individual intelligence, personality, skill, and the substance of discussions—combined." Exemplary cases of peak-performing teams describe energy and connections in conversations inside and, importantly, outside formal meetings.

If the "how" is healthy communication, the "who" is the foundation. The highest-performing teams are internally motivated, persistent through frustration, can delay immediate gratification for longer-term success, and regulate their moods to maintain a healthy culture. Elite teams are served by leaders to enter difficult conversations and dissenting voices. They bring out the very best in their peers and are in alignment. And it pays dividends. Research by Scott Keller and Mary Meaney observed that when teams align on a common vision, they are almost twice as likely to deliver above-median financial performance.[139]

We are not capable of becoming elite unless we foster curiosity, and context is expanded. High performers normally have a broader understanding of context surrounding them, including exposure to diverse challenges, people, competitive threats, and customer requests. The highest-performing teams are more well rounded and comprised of diverse and varied viewpoints.

Elite organizations understand their calling, their team's assets, and their unique communication styles. This self-analysis is meant to drive the best from each other. They ask a different question: "Where do we need to focus, and what do we need to learn in order to become distinct and elite?"

WHAT NOW?

When does your lack of internal motivation show up? What does it cost you, and what one thing can you practice today to build a healthy, internally inspired team?

"Great things in business are never done by one person; they're done by a team of people."

STEVE JOBS

80/20 EVERYTHING

"The way to create something great
is to create something simple."

RICHARD KOCH

I like to start many of my forum events with a challenge: "There will be many big ideas shared today, but only one or two are worth taking action on right now. Your challenge is to figure out which ideas are meant for you and are actionable today." Varying studies show that we are exposed to over two thousand daily marketing messages, all competing for our attention. Our favorite coping mechanism is the "to-do" list because it helps us stay organized. But does it help us make better decisions? It's a wish list, not a priority list. Is your to-do list so big it takes you away from the bigger personal goals or dreams that inspire you? If so, you need extreme clarity.

Researcher and author Cal Newport states that optimal performance takes place during "Deep Work": a state of distraction-free concentration, pushing cognitive abilities to their limit and actively generating new value with less effort.[140] It's no wonder the Deep Work paradigm is so important. The average person gets interrupted every eight minutes, seven times an hour or fifty-six times a day. The average interruption lasts five minutes, which means one can spend up to five hours a day distracted. And here is where it gets interesting: almost 80 percent of those interruptions create "little or no value." Three hours of time is wasted per day.

We are losing ourselves in a whirlwind of interruptions and impulsive "low-value" priorities. Activity doesn't necessarily result in accomplishment. Here's more proof:

- Ninety-five percent of self-improvement books and tapes purchased are not used.

- Ninety percent daydream in meetings because 50 percent of meetings are unproductive.

- Ninety percent of what we read is not retained.

We need to simplify our approach to work and mental concentration. But, more importantly, we need to simplify our approach to *what we concentrate on*. Mental concentration is the battle, but prioritization is the war.

Artist, musician, and entrepreneur Dr. Dre shared that after working ten years on a musical project, he tossed it. He explained that it simply "was not good," and instead he chose to focus on his album, *Compton*. He chose what was relevant to him rather than what would water down his impressive musical catalogue.

This is also one of Steve Jobs's mantras: "Focus and simplicity. Simple can be harder than complex: You must work hard to get your thinking clean to make it simple. But it's worth it in the end because once you get there, you can move mountains."[141]

Most activities and meetings don't assist you in moving mountains; they stagnate, decelerate, and create growth slowdowns. John Kenneth Galbraith was prophetic when he quipped, "Meetings are indispensable when you don't want to do anything."[142] Sadly, most projects, meetings, and base activities need to be neutralized because they are not part of the critical few steps that matter.

My friend and entrepreneur Perry Marshall has spent the last twenty years researching, studying, and applying the principles embedded in Pareto's 80/20 principle. He conveys in his book *80/20 Sales and Marketing* that "we're all tempted to waste our time trying to please all of our customers instead of the most lucrative ones. We are all conditioned to always respond to the stimulus around us. So, if you obey the 80/20 rule, you are always going to feel as though you are ignoring something—because you are."[143]

Marshall reminds us that "all customers are not equal. Far from it. Some earn you an amazingly disproportionate amount of money, many make you a little bit of money, and some even waste your time. With the last group, you lose money selling anything to them at all." Offering your products or services to the right person is more important the any sales strategy. The wrong prospect isn't open to your ideas.

Where are you investing way too much time into something that will never provide a return?

What we forget is that there's an 80/20 within the 80/20. Or 64 percent of the value is attributed to 4 percent of the work or activities. And if we go one step deeper, 51.2 percent of the value is attributable to only 0.8 percent of the work or activities. Could it be that 1 percent of your decisions drive 50 percent of the value created? How could you:

- Go deeper with the 1 percent of your customers, yielding 50 percent of your success?

- Neutralize the 1 percent of customers creating 50 percent of your headaches?

- Systemize the 1 percent of your challenges that account for 50 percent of your problems?

Richard Koch, entrepreneur and author of *The 80/20 Principle: The Secret to Achieving More with Less*, states, "80% of the results come from 20% of the causes. A few things are important; most are not."[144] The 80/20 principle or "the law of the few" can't be ignored. Not all customers are equal, and not all initiatives deserve your full attention.

> **Not all customers are equal, and not all initiatives deserve your full attention.**

There's always an unbalanced return on a few big decisions.

There is nothing but opportunity all around us. If 80 percent of anything contributes 20 percent of the value, then there are way too many under-performing resources that need to be redirected toward something much more productive.

Which projects, customers, and people deserve your full attention?

WHAT NOW?

When do feelings of overwhelm show up? What do they cost you, and what one thing can you practice today to focus on the 20 percent of activities that matter most?

"Out of clutter, find simplicity."

ALBERT EINSTEIN

THREE OF FOUR MEETINGS FAIL

"The longer the meeting, the less is accomplished."

TIM COOK

I recently sat through a meeting that put me in a trance. The objective was unclear, and the meeting was poorly facilitated and packed with too much information. As I looked around the room, I observed that everyone looked exhausted, unmotivated, and disengaged. The meeting leader had not conveyed a cohesive story and had failed to deliver on the objective of the meeting. Poorly led meetings occur at epidemic levels, which is why 90 percent of people daydream during these sessions.[145] Most attendees are not present, are working on other projects, or are not engaging in the discussion at hand. When attentions start to drift, the meeting has already failed.

Meetings are one of the most universally accepted time wasters in the modern workplace. Almost everyone can recall a time when they walked out of a meeting and thought, "Please just shoot me an email next time." According to a survey of almost two hundred senior executives conducted by Steven Rogelberg of the University of North Carolina, 71 percent of meetings are "unproductive and ineffective" while a similar number felt meetings kept them from doing necessary work.[146] Most people say they normally do other work during meetings, and of those who don't, many are checked out and unfocused on the topic at hand.

The first and most easily avoidable mistake is the badly timed meeting. There's a time and a place for meetings, yet sometimes leaders disregard the needs of teammates and schedule gatherings focusing on their own convenience. When a teammate has a mountain of individual work, they'll be mentally checked out before the meeting even begins. Remember, a meeting is a transaction of another's time and energy. Do you assess the needs and interests of your coworkers, or are you stealing their most valuable moments?

Meetings are ill prepared, scheduled far too often, and many times result in mundane, time-wasting conversation instead of creativity and collaboration. Consider this: set aside time for the most important topics to be discussed, and if the information can be conveyed without any input from the team, then reconsider the necessity of the meeting. The most productive meetings focus on discussion, debate, and critique, not information dumps.

The most productive meetings focus on discussion, debate, and critique, not information dumps.

Often, the biggest personalities monopolize conversations, hijacking broader discussions and rambling to disguise the fact that they are unprepared. Roger Schwarz, an organizational psychologist and author of *Smart Leaders, Smarter Teams*, reminds us: "You're there to be a steward of all the ideas in the room."[147] You want "participants to see the team meeting as a puzzle—their role is to get the pieces out on the table and figure out how they fit together," says Schwarz. These types of conversations harness the wisdom of the room, focusing on value communication and strategy prioritization.

What are the secrets of creating a winning meeting?

1. Research shows that we have an attention span of ten to eighteen minutes per topic, or the length of a good TED Talk. All meetings should start with the leader answering the questions, "Why are we here, and what needs to be solved?" At the beginning of each meeting, the leader must state if they are looking for additional input and validation or if they are sharing a topic that is already finalized.

2. Most meetings are comprised of too many topics and not enough emphasis on the application and pitfalls of the idea in question. The best team gatherings have no more than three topics, and every attendee walks away with crystal-clear next steps. If you don't own a "next step," you shouldn't be at the meeting.

3. It's not an overstatement to say the first minute of any presentation is the most important for both personal momentum and audience engagement. Within the first sixty seconds, it's vital to capture the audience's attention, but as any presenter can attest, the concentration of a room full of distracted people is difficult to manage. In your first minute, try to paint a picture of the problem for your audience. If you're able to harness the audience's emotions, they'll be much more invested as the presentation moves forward.

4. Going into a presentation with a pitch mentality can be a big misstep. Structural planning is obviously important for success, but often presenters are too long winded and rigid. Utilize improvisation, and don't be fearful of going off script. People connect much more deeply when they feel like you're talking *with* them, not *at* them.

5. When information is fired at you in quick succession without letting the conversation breathe, the audience will often check out. Slow the delivery of content down, and try to let the audience simmer on an idea before moving on to the next topic. Take the opportunity to personalize the message by asking for input from anyone within the team. These conversational breaths are opportunities to glean wisdom from the group and make the meeting less of a lecture and more of a back-and-forth dialogue.

A director of a play facilitates the production from behind the stage. They pull out the very best of their performers. If your teammates don't walk out of a meeting contributing, inspired, and clear on their purpose, the meeting missed the mark. The most successful meetings are like good theatre.

WHAT NOW?

When do you waste others' time with irrelevant information? What does it cost you, and what one thing can you practice today to design inspirational meetings?

"Meetings are a symptom of bad organization.
The fewer meetings the better."

PETER DRUCKER

HUMAN EXPERIENCES CREATE LOYALTY

"Great vision without great people is irrelevant."

JIM COLLINS

My friend Craig Dubitsky, founder and CEO of Hello Products, had a dream of changing the way the world thinks about toothpaste, mouthwash, and oral health. His desire was to create the Apple brand of oral care. His solution was Hello Products, a "naturally friendly oral care" portfolio that transformed the oral care category similarly to other brands he was associated with in his past, including Method Products and Eos Products. Craig Dubitsky is jovial, engaging, and lovingly irreverent. He is a walking, talking personal experience, and he created a brand in his own image. Hello Products greets you from the shelf with bold graphics and compelling colors. He created so much momentum so quickly that Colgate-Palmolive Company announced it was acquiring Hello Products and asked Craig to continue as a creator and partner. Human experiences create loyalty, emotional connection, and relationships with consumers. An organization's authentic humanity and optimism is a force multiplier.

Talent and passion are the difference; it's the great equalizer. Research fielded by Brent Adamson and Matthew Dixon validates this argument. They found that the sales experience created by passionate (emotionally committed) salespeople accounts for 53 percent of the customer loyalty—more than brand relevance, shipping efficiency, and price/value ratio combined![148] A good product, shipped on time, priced right, only gets you in the game. The people selling, serving, nurturing, and blanketing the customer experience are the deciding factor. The research shows that the talent composition of a team is the most important factor in any organization. So, what are the behaviors of these special sales evangelists?

According to Adamson and Dixon's research, the highest-performing sales and service providers are teachers of new information (not sellers) and they challenge their customers' view of the world. They love to confront norms and encourage creative tension. They recognize that this discomfort is necessary to encourage someone to move in a new direction. They embrace the idea that change requires discomfort. And they are not afraid of it.

The customer already knows your product offering; new value occurs when you teach them how to operate their business better. How are you at sharing transformational insights with your customer or helping them understand competitive threats or emerging risks in their business?

> **The customer already knows your product offering; new value occurs when you teach them how to operate their business better.**

The goal is not just creating healthy partnerships but to become "memorable." Researchers and business advisors Matthew Dixon and Brent Adamson suggest three ideas to be memorable in your customers' eyes.

TEACH. Memorable partners share customized "insight-led" conversations. To quote the authors: "Differentiate yourself by showing your customer something new about their industry that they didn't know or provide them with a different view." The best "teach" by conveying fresh viewpoints that include advanced philosophies, growth strategies, or new models.

TENSION. The top sales organizations are highly relational; they are candid, forthright, and honest about business challenges. The authors state that the most valuable customer engagements cause slight discomfort. This occurs when one's views are challenged, but often one will reassess their views. Each challenging discussion should be tailored to the customer's strategic agenda and personal buying preferences.

COURAGE. Most sales organizations are fearful of creating tension in a customer discussion. Think about it: your most intimate connections occasionally have moments of strain and debate. Should your top customer relationships be any different? Don't be timid to share how similar companies took a wrong turn, opening themselves up to competitive threats. The best sales organizations have the courage to confront the root challenges that hinder growth.

These elite leaders encourage others to look at the world in a fresh way. And they thrive on hearing the words, "Wow, I have never looked at it that way before."

Finally, they are very gifted at communicating and exhibiting a presence that clearly demonstrates "why" you should purchase and partner with them. They streamline ideas, connect dots, are empathetic listeners, understand their customer's unstated (emotional) concerns, and are comfortable helping the customer navigate decisions and risks. Their special identity (and passion for service) is on display for the world to see. It jumps out at you and cannot be ignored.

Their customer service **IS** the brand experience. I saw this trait many times at the meeting I attended. The best in the room exhibits these traits, and their firm hires for these traits. That is why this company has benefitted from 20 to 30 percent growth for five straight years. Do you have the right people representing your team, and are you always on the lookout for experiential talent?

WHAT NOW?

When does your failure to create emotional experiences with others show up? What does it cost you, and what one thing can you practice today to illustrate experiential leadership with others?

"Greatness, it turns out, is largely a matter
of conscious choice, and discipline."

JIM COLLINS

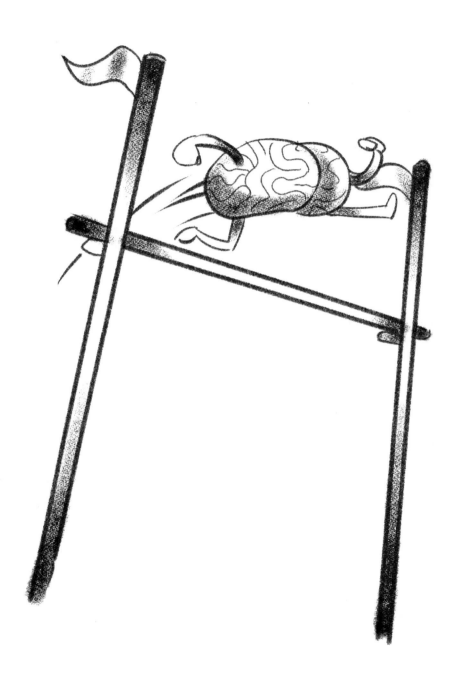

HOW AGILE ARE YOU REALLY?

"Should you fail to pilot your own ship, don't be surprised at what inappropriate port you find yourself docked."

TOM ROBBINS

"Dan, you're not going to believe this update. The electricity just went out in the hotel, and the whole block is dark. The energy source has been knocked out, and the hotel has no idea when the juice will be back on. I have no idea what to tell you."

It was 8:45 a.m. in Las Vegas, and I was doing some deep breathing prior to walking out on a stage in front of 150 associates who had purchased tickets to be part of an exclusive growth summit featuring leaders from Google, IDEO, Walgreens, Amazon, Rite Aid, IRI, and Nielsen. I walked over to one of my business partners and said, "What now?" The bottom had fallen out of event, and the rules immediately changed. As we all stood in a half-lit hotel, it hit me. How do we reframe this moment to serve us?

Our plan was to go gather fifty candles from the front desk, and to have all 150 people move much closer together in a circle, creating an informal retreat atmosphere, with each of the speakers speaking without audiovisual support, having to informally discuss their ideas, allowing for audience participation. Our plan was to use the crisis as a moment to have real, unscripted discussion with the audience. The goal was an event that was raw, unrehearsed, and vulnerable.

As I walked to the front of the room and started sharing our plan with the audience, the lights almost magically went on at 9:00 a.m., which was our planned start time. The lights coming back on was almost as disruptive as the lights going out. I started to laugh, grabbed the microphone, and explained to the audience our plan was to improvise and create an unfiltered conference, but now we are going back to the safety of our initial program. To this day, I would have loved to have seen how the candlelit conference would have progressed. We dramatically pivoted, out of necessity, but there was something very human and alive about that fifteen-minute experience. How agile are you really?

Speed, digital transformation, and emerging competitive threats are transforming most industries, and agility is no longer a luxury; it's a necessity. Recent research by Deloitte and McKinsey uncovered that 90 percent of senior leaders highly value organizational agility, but only 10 percent see their team as agile.[149] This gap begs the question: Why are so many firms inflexible?

"The Fourth Industrial Revolution" describes the phase of history following the Automation Revolution and states that after humans automate our technology, we seek to integrate it into our lives, our jobs, and even into ourselves.[150] Just a few years after the term took center stage at 2016 Davos, it returned as the primary theme of this year's event. Change is happening and happening quickly, and it impacts every part of our lives.

A generation ago, we believed we could anticipate future moves. We now know we must practice contingency planning, course correction, and fast pivots as we encounter challenges. The extent of this change means we must all get comfortable not knowing the answers to many of the questions surrounding us. But building an agile mindset is of a shockingly low priority with most organizations. In a recent study conducted by Frost and Sullivan for Pegasystems, 20 percent of executives surveyed said they view business agility as central in their business strategy, and only 43 percent call themselves adopters of agility.[151]

> **Change is happening and happening quickly, and it impacts every part of our lives.**

Many organizations that had not adopted an agile approach appeared to be risk averse. This same study stated four of ten respondents lacked experience with agile methods. Additionally, they lacked leadership support and believed agile practices cost too much for it to be worth the tradeoff. Meanwhile, those who adopted an agile mindset saw noticeable increases in revenue, profit, customer satisfaction, and retention.

WHAT IS THE MAGIC OF AGILITY?

Over the past decade, even Walmart has modeled how agility is an enabler for transformation. When they acquired Jet.com in 2016, they invited Jet's founder Marc Lore to lead the Walmart digital platform. Within a year, they infused an entrepreneurial mindset into their traditional model. Walmart now embraces speed, experimentation, and agility, driving stronger consumer experiences, loyalty, and growth. When you are large and flexible, you become even more dangerous to your competition.

THREE IDEAS TO BECOME MORE AGILE.

1. Consider creating a rogue "war-room" mentality within your organization. Google historically allowed 20 percent of their associates time to be dedicated to new ideas, pet projects, and their own innovations.[152] Are you courageous enough to embrace this philosophy?

2. Agile teams embrace faster decisions through "scrums" (daily communications with flexible reassessment), "sprints" (short-term projects to test new items, processes, and improvements), and "stand-up meetings" (focusing on updates and action steps). These strategies are meant to generate an entrepreneurial mindset and eliminate wasted time.

3. Do you encourage your team to make quick decisions, lead process improvements, and eliminate outdated tasks within your organization? Agile cultures don't have the time (or bandwidth) to lead all change initiatives from the top down. Agility requires trust, and it must be practiced on a granular level. Can your leaders pull the trigger on decisions without three levels of approval?

A recent *Forbes* article states that we can't get comfortable once we've tasted success. "The world moves way too fast and technology is too much of a game-changer to ever think you can settle into one way of approaching your business … If you look at your business as an experiment, you will never fail: you're just working on the right formula."[153]

WHAT NOW?

When does your lack of risk aversion show up? What does it cost you, and what one thing can you practice today to epitomize more agility, flexibility, and comfort with change?

"The agile way is more adapt to changes
but shall not lose the sight of big picture."

PEARL ZHU

THE SECRETS OF COCREATION

"It is the long history of humankind (and animal kind, too) that those who learned to collaborate and improvise most effectively have prevailed."

CHARLES DARWIN

As DenTek Oral Care's leader of sales, I was responsible for brand development in all major retailers in the US and Canada. It taught me the necessity of cocreation with major retailers such as Walmart, Target, Walgreens, and CVS Health. DenTek was a small, privately held company in Tennessee and one of the leaders in dental accessories and specialty oral health. They were off the radar, keenly entrepreneurial, and aggressive.

John Jansheski founded DenTek in 1984, turning his dentist father's dental pick invention into an oral care empire that eventually sold for over $200 million, competing against the likes of P&G, Church & Dwight, Colgate-Palmolive, and GlaxoSmithKline. DenTek possessed the broadest assortment of floss picks, interdental brushes, dental repair, and mouth guards for teeth grinding—but their real skill was how they openly engaged retailers, exploring their unmet needs and partnering with them on the design of customized and often exclusive items. Their skills at cocreation with Walmart, Target, Walgreens, and CVS Health established preferred relationships that set them apart from many of their larger competitors. John Jansheski created a listening culture that thrived on looking for new product ideas that could be codesigned with his retail partners, outmaneuvering his competition.

You can't ignore cocreation if you want to succeed. Research shows that 70 percent of companies that deliver best-in-class customer experience use customer feedback.[154] When the customer is involved in the innovation process, a better solution is always created. The cocreation philosophy works and is expanding as consumers get younger, demanding personalized solutions.

Eighty-one percent of millennials would be interested in helping a brand or company design a new product.[155] Allowing codevelopment toward a solution encourages commitment and scratches the innovation itch we all possess.

Cocreation (or collaborative innovation) is when an organization carves out space to work with their partners and customers on innovation. All cocreation experiences are built on three practices: a) transparent sharing of ideas; b) the involvement of the consumer; c) discovering or improving new innovations.

We see this today modeled through YouTube's user-generated content, Wikipedia's mass collaboration, and Target's exclusive, custom innovation model. In each of these trends, the consumer is involved, there are limited boundaries, and it's disruptive.

The fathers of the idea of cocreation are researchers C. K. Prahalad and Venkat Ramaswamy. Early on, they argued that the future of competitive advantage would be the art of cocreation. Organizations must be flexible, agile, collaborative, boundaryless, and astute at the knowledge transfer within.[156]

The benefits of cocreation are significant: consumers receive personalized solutions; retailers offer brands or services that make them distinct; and brands turn new knowledge from customers into something that differentiates them from their competitors. The cocreation mindset expands organizational boundaries, encouraging a more curious, innovative culture. The process encourages

Organizations must be flexible, agile, collaborative, boundaryless, and astute at the knowledge transfer within.

loyalty, generating more ideas than transactional engagements; it encourages deeper relationships and facilitates creativity. How do the best codevelop solutions with their customers?

UNCOMMON INSIGHTS. They draw on a combination of insights, marketing ideas, emerging trends, design prototypes, and thoughtful discovery questions, forging deeper innovation discussions.

FACILITATED DISCUSSIONS. They engage in discovery, curiosity, and trend evaluation to uncover future needs and align joint interests. They have fun with the process and are experiential.

MUTUAL LEARNING. Knowledge is shared, ideas are discovered, and expectations and follow-up meetings are agreed to upfront.

PEOPLE AND PURPOSE. Intent is clear with the right people in the room. Roles are clear to optimize the process.

Although internal research and marketing departments are essential to uncovering growth ideas, the impact of their ideas can be magnified once they step out of their echo chamber into the customer's world.

The wisdom of crowds reminds us that two heads are always better than one.

WHAT NOW?

When does your lack of collaboration show up? What does it cost you, and what one thing can you practice today to truly cocreate with your partners?

"Politeness is the poison of collaboration."

EDWIN LAND

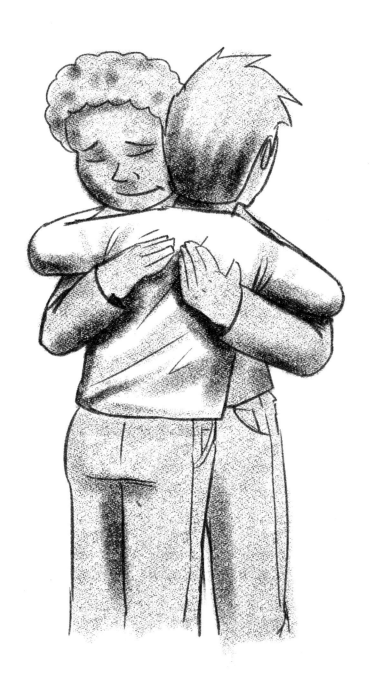

THE SOUL OF A CULTURE

"The great challenge of adulthood is holding on to
  your idealism after you lose your innocence."

BRUCE SPRINGSTEEN

Starbucks's CEO Howard Schultz once shared, "Success is not sustainable if it's defined by how big you become or by growth for growth's sake. Success is very shallow if it doesn't have emotional meaning."[157] Schultz didn't just want to build a coffee company; he wanted to "build a company that my father never got a chance to work for." Organizations with soul attract the eyes of the consumers and often are its most compelling asset. The research shows that people leave bosses, not companies, and consumers will discard a brand because they disagree with the social views of the founder. Soul-searching continues to grow in importance with us all.

Zingerman's Deli was previously named "The Coolest Small Company in America" by *Inc.* magazine. This two-floor deli in Ann Arbor, Michigan, had turned twenty-one when it received this praiseworthy award. As Bo Burlingham wrote in his book, *Small Giants*, they "chose to be great instead of big."[158]

Zingerman's has been a case study for brilliant branding and is a company that has held steadfast to their story, remaining authentic. But their internal structure is what's truly amazing. When Zingerman's decided to expand on their business practices, they chose to partner with independent businesses and services rather than the typical franchise expansion model. They have an Open Book Management philosophy, and it works so well that one of their many corporate limbs is a consulting group that teaches the secrets of their culture. Open Book Management requires every employee to think, lead, and act like owners of the company. According to research done by Denison Consulting Group, companies using Open Book Management are in the top 10 percent of corporate cultures.[159] It is daring, and it works.

What's the soul of your company? It's not created; it's uncovered. The most attractive organizations are fueled by story, embracing a calling other than padding the bottom line. These special organizations create meaning for all involved. I have worked with many companies that were financially productive but not significant. The most significant organizations are driven by a calling, shared values, and soul!

> **The most attractive organizations are fueled by story, embracing a calling other than padding the bottom line.**

Many organizations are short on soul. But if you look, you'll find it in the most unlikely places. You find it in businesses, teams, and the arts. You find it with Springsteen.

The story goes: Springsteen uncovered deeper purpose shortly after the 1980 "The River" tour. He shares, "I thought perhaps mapping ... the distance between the American dream and American reality might be my service, one I could provide that would accompany the entertainment and the good times I brought my fans. I hoped it might give roots and mission to our band."[160] Part of his mission has been to chronicle the "gap" between the American dream and the American reality.

During this era of refining his work, he discovered his mission. He was pregnant with this idea for more than a decade but gave birth to it only after it was fully formed. Purpose is normally not discovered; it's uncovered. And its running mate is self-doubt.

Springsteen's story is filled with an inner spirit yet embraces bouts of depression, anxiety, and inconsistencies coupled with waves of self-doubt. A larger calling animates the band, his music, and his writing. I see this with numerous companies that I admire: Kind, Chobani, Warby Parker, Seventh Generation, Sundial Brands, Starbucks, Zingerman's Delicatessen, and Father Greg Boyle, founder of Homeboy Industries in Los Angeles, the largest gang-intervention, rehabilitation, and reentry program in the world.

We are starved for companies with a soul: organizations that have created meaning, financial vitality, and a culture that pulls out the best in their associates. Does your organization have soul?

WHAT NOW?

When does your lack of team soul show up? What does it cost you, and what one thing can you practice today to bring *soul* to your team?

"At the end of every hard-earned day, people
find some reason to believe."

BRUCE SPRINGSTEEN

A LIKEABLE COMPANY

"Listen first and never stop listening."

DAVE KERPEN

As my family knows, there is not a mechanical or technical attribute in my body. I was truly skipped over when these skills were being doled out. On a good day I can replace a lightbulb or change the batteries in the fire detector. That's why I love Bob, our longtime handyman. For years, Bob would drop in and work his magic, effortlessly working through the repair list and bringing to life things we never even realized were damaged. Bob supplied me with an invaluable utility, but what I valued most about Bob was his riveting company.

Bob was a recovering alcoholic who gained great pride in extremely overdelivering on his services, solving concealed messes, and addressing them before they blossomed into bigger headaches. Bob would also work with apprentices who had veered off the road as younger men, like himself. He would walk around our house, looking for things to fix and would encourage me with his words. This man taught me more with his actions and psychology than any book on leadership. I simply liked Bob, valued his services, and was inspired by everything his company stood for. He was experiential, trustworthy, and likeable.

Many of today's most compelling companies don't just sell products; they create emotionally connected relationships with their customers. These organizations are ecosystems aligned around designing lifestyle brands that consumers emotionally carry within them, and they are extremely likeable. Their organizations uncover and solve buried problems customers may not even be aware of yet. Resolving problems is never a burden to them; in fact, it is a moment to demonstrate values, build loyalty, and deepen relationships.

Companies that are invested in customer intimacy are often described as "likeable" organizations. The difficulty arises when we seek to fabricate likeability, rather than invest in deeply healthy leaders and habits. As management consultant Steve Tobak pointed out in an *Entrepreneur* article, "The problem with likability as a goal or metric is that it's highly subjective: one person's jerk is another person's loving spouse, best friend or great boss. It's also highly situational: everyone is a jerk some of the time, depending on the situation and how they're treated by others."[161]

Likeability may be innately personal, but everyone knows it when they see it. It's the outflow of high emotional intelligence that includes self-awareness, empathy, humility, and reliability.

Individuals may not always win by being respected, but they will almost certainly lose if they are not likeable. Black Swan, a negotiation-training agency, says people are six times more likely to do business with someone they like.[162] Likeability is a compelling characteristic that creates team cohesion and guides talent and new customers. How often have you seen leaders removed

One may have short-term success while not being liked, but rarely will they have long-term success.

from their senior assignment because others can't stand to be in their presence?

Whether it's a self-awareness problem or a lack of humility, the distrust of bad leaders permeates too many organizations. One may have short-term success while not being liked, but rarely will they have long-term success.

A house built on sand …

THE TRAITS

Want to be a likeable company? Try repairing things. This includes putting right relationships, clearing up misunderstandings, and keeping promises with associates. Lee Resources conducted a study and discovered that organizations that resolve a complaint in the customer's favor create an emotional bond; the consumer is 70 percent more likely to do business again with that firm.[163] In a world that rarely delivers on a promise, dependability is irresistible.

Do you want to be a respected and likeable leader? Honestly pursue (and listen to) personal feedback. Research by Jack Zenger and Joseph Folkman found that "leaders who ask for feedback are better liked and more effective than those who don't." Similarly, the research uncovered that only one in two thousand "unlikeable leaders" are thought to be effective.[164] The traits that greatly increased one's likability include:

1. Having positive emotional connections with others, protecting relationships, and reaching out to teammates who feel disconnected from the broader group.

2. Being a truth-teller and a concise communicator, giving credit to others, inspiring confidence.

3. Asking for feedback and being willing to personally look in the mirror, own mistakes, and change.

Bob, my "fix-it" guy, was much more than a repair specialist. He was the archetype of what a high-performing service company should aspire to become. He mastered listening, serving, and empathizing. Yes, Bob addressed broken things within our home, but he also left an emotional deposit with everyone who called him for services. Every time Bob finished a job, he left a remnant of his caring and personality behind. I looked forward to accumulating problems on my "fix-it" list so he would drop by and see us again. Is your team known for leaving an imprint, or an echo of your caring, and are you likeable?

WHAT NOW?

When does your apathy show up? What does it cost you, and what one thing can you practice today to show positive intent and likeability to associates, customers, and your peers?

"We are far more revealing by the questions we ask than the answers we give. Answer briefly to sense where their questions are heading."

KARE ANDERSON

DARK HORSES DISRUPT

"When the ideas are coming, I don't stop until the ideas
stop because that train doesn't come along all the time."

DR. DRE

I always have my eyes open for dark horses, the come-from-behind winners that no one expects. A few years back, I started interviewing smaller, purpose-driven companies that were winning despite their size. Dark horse companies frequently have limited financial coffers, little brand awareness, and none of the cushion that comes with historic success. Against all odds, they win anyway. People see themselves as dark horses in many aspects of their life, which makes underdog brands more relatable, more familiar, and more effective than ever.

Gone are the days of big companies outperforming the small. Today, most industries are being shaped by emerging smaller and midsized organizations, many of which out-innovate competitors that are much larger and more powerful. According to an IRI report, small and medium manufacturers accounted for more than 75 percent of all "New Product Pacesetter" companies and 64 percent of the growth in dollars.[165]

> **Today, most industries are being shaped by emerging smaller and midsized organizations.**

New disruptive, challenger brands are having a profound impact on business and the broader culture.

Sales for many of the leading packaged food organizations are not stellar. With a few exceptions, most of the top consumer packaged goods companies are growing at all-time low levels. They are not innovating. But why?

According to recent research by Goldman, larger brands still control the lion's share of the business (close to 80 percent), but smaller, emerging challenger companies have the edge, gaining share in 62 percent of the top fifty packaged food categories.[166] Are they more innovative, and do they understand the heart of the new consumer better than their competitors?

Consumers love to discover early-stage brands with unique identities and purpose. Brands like KIND, Olly Nutrition, Ripple, Zevia, Vita Coco, CREMO, and Hello Brands are masters of marrying purpose with experiential branding and distinct formulations. They introduce innovation in uncrowded spaces within the category. Or they create new categories altogether.

They also listen intently to their core customers. If they uncover a new need in their ongoing customer discussions, they codevelop a product for them immediately. They are one with their tribe. When they see a problem, they fix it immediately. And when they uncover a white space, they fill it.

According to a report in CircleUp, larger companies are sometimes calling new packaging or line extensions "innovation." The report further states that some of the largest CPG companies "spend up to six times more on marketing and advertising of old products than they do on innovation of new products. Of that innovation, only 39 percent are new products, while the other 61 percent are incremental changes to existing products."[167] Let's be honest: another flavor is not innovation.

Entrepreneurial founders think differently. I am reminded of the five years of research and interviews I conducted for my first book, *Dark Horse: How Challenger Companies Rise to Prominence*. Smaller, emerging companies that outthink and out inspire their competition embrace ten traits:[168]

1. Their business is personal, it's an extension of their identity, and it's about more than profit.

2. They listen well and stay in deep alignment with top customers.

3. They use their organization's hidden intangible assets to create differentiating value.

4. They create a clear, vibrant business blueprint and share it passionately with their community.

5. They carefully and wisely pick their customers and their partners.

6. They cocreate innovation with customers, becoming more valuable for the customers.

7. They understand cultural shifts and experientially meet the consumer where they are at.

8. They authentically build consumer community, and these influencers help build their brand.

9. They are very agile and nimble and seize new opportunities much faster than competitors.

10. Their corporate culture engages the consumer with a spirit of grace and likeability.

Maybe it's time to start thinking more like a tech company. The average tech company dedicates 15 percent of the investments to R&D, while CPG only commits 2 or 3 percent.[169] There is too much wasted investment in underperforming overhead and not enough in experimentation, customer experience, cutting packages and one-on-one relationships passionately listening, building an intimate customer relationship.

WHAT NOW?

When does your lack of grit show up? What does it cost you, and what one thing can you practice today to disrupt the status quo?

"Brands are trying to become more like people and people are trying to become brands."

BLAIR EADIE

THE POWER OF YOUR BRAIN TRUST

"If you aren't experiencing failure, then you
are making a far worse mistake: You are
being driven by the desire to avoid it."

ED CATMULL

Historically, I would spend hours preparing to moderate roundtable discussions with diverse groups of senior executives. I would present emerging trends, new research, best practices, and lots of provocative questions meant to elicit personal reflection and engagement within the forum community. I mistakenly believed my role was to be the primary educator and inspiration of the gathering, but I quickly realized that the participants contributed a collective insight that was far more valuable than any personal contribution. This is the power of your brain trust. Some of the wisest leaders I know are experts at harnessing the whole room. They thoughtfully create a brain trust of advisors to test ideas prior to finalizing their thinking. The smartest person in the room is always the room.

In the last twenty years, only two of Pixar's twenty films have flopped. They have created some of the most successful, innovative, and commercially relevant films of the last two decades (*Toy Story*,

Monsters, Inc., *Finding Nemo*, *The Incredibles*, *Up*, *Brave*, and *WALL-E*). How have they done it? Ed Catmull, cofounder of Pixar Animation, says it's simple: the brain trust.

The smartest person in the room is always the room.

In his bestseller, *Creativity Inc.*, Catmull says, "For all the care you put into artistry, visual polish frequently doesn't matter if you are getting the story right."[170]

Brain trusts are comprised of advisors whose only concern is leading someone to their most optimal outcome. Their analysis is unaffected by external forces, and they care deeply about a project's success—enough to be completely candid about problems. Catmull states that brain trusts are excellent at "stripping down a story to its emotional, load-bearing sequences and then rebuilding it from the ground up." They are engineers of objectivity, and they are essential to one's strategy.

A necessary element to a successful brain trust is a healthy candor. As Catmull has said, "We believe that ideas—and thus, films—only become great when they are challenged and tested." An effective brain trust eliminates hierarchy and power figures in the group, assessing the creative process (or art), not the artist.

The best brain trusts enlist people who offer a unique vantage point; who are open, progressive, and healthy leaders; who address broader solutions. Effective brain trusts liberate us. We are all prisoners of our personal biases.

WE ALL NEED A BRAIN TRUST.

Maybe the biggest blind spot in leadership is the illusion that wanting to see clearly is the same thing as seeing clearly. I frequently work with leaders who care deeply about being sound in their reasoning and receptive to critique. This is something we should always strive for, but it isn't enough. Personal biases affect our reasoning, which is why we need a brain trust.

Robert Cialdini, Regents' Professor Emeritus of Psychology and Marketing at Arizona State, reminds us that "we all fool ourselves from time to time to keep our thoughts and beliefs consistent with what we have already done or decided."[171] Our need to stay consistent with our views of ourselves is a very powerful motivating force.

A brain trust works to dismantle our instincts. Here are some of the biases a brain trust can help us overcome:

CONFIRMATION BIAS. We look for ideas to confirm our own personal views.

IN-GROUP BIAS. We often favor people who are like us.

SOCIAL PROOF. We are influenced by people with title, power, or influence.

We all suffer from personal biases, and a trusted brain trust allows you to see through others' eyes. Who are the core members of your brain trust?

WHAT NOW?

When do your personal biases show up? What do they cost you, and what one thing can you practice today to be more coachable and teachable?

"You are not your idea, and if you identify too closely with your ideas, you will take offense when they are challenged."

ED CATMULL

LESSONS FROM "THE DEAD"

"Be yourself; everyone else is already taken."

OSCAR WILDE

The Grateful Dead were never a band with numerous Billboard hits, entering the Top 40 only once with "Touch of Grey." They were a rock band, but deep down saw themselves as a jazz ensemble inspired by Miles Davis and other improvisational artists. They never played a song the same way twice and incorporated live improvisation into everything they created. They were vulnerable because of it. "They'll follow me down any dark alley," Garcia noted in 1987. "Sometimes there's a light at the end of the tunnel, and sometimes there's a dark hole. The point is, you don't get adventure in music unless you're willing to take chances." Vulnerability is not a fluffy idea; it is the heart of risk taking.

> **Vulnerability is not a fluffy idea; it is the heart of risk taking.**

Most companies are guilty of playing a perpetual game of "follow the leader," reading the same business books, going to the same conferences, and making the same mistakes. That is why the misfits and outsiders can sneak up and steal the show with innovative ideas or new ways of thinking. What lessons can we learn from a band that was fifty years ahead of their time? Let's ponder the lessons of The Grateful Dead.

IMPROVISATION. The essence of improvisation means taking what is unexpected or disruptive and using it to your advantage. The Grateful Dead—like all jam bands—played off each other in the moment, adapting and following each other's lead. This genre of music ignores hierarchy and rigidity. It's a constant process of taking and giving back the melody, letting the inspired member lead.

COCREATION. Amazingly, The Dead captured the admiration of their tribe within their music and outside of it. Barry Barnes explains: "Long before Facebook, Deadheads created their own dispersed social network, a tribe of fans united by a love of the band's music and a commitment to its values. This community formed the foundation of the band's business model."[172] Starting in the '60s, "The Dead did precisely what the internet is encouraging today—erasing the boundaries between producer and consumer. Their fans created a genuinely collaborative environment in which both produced the organization's greatest product—the live concert performance." The focus was always on a symbiotic cocreation with their fans.

Recording was allowed at all live performances, with the caveat of sharing or trading with other fans. "They recognized that this grew their fan base, while creating a historical record as every show was different." And the band's makeshift newsletter (the signup printed on a 1971 album) grew to nearly one hundred thousand people in ten years. It was organic, communal—and, most of all, inclusive. The Dead understood that cocreation starts with an invitation.

Outside of every Dead show were entire economies of hunter-gatherers that traveled with the band. The Dead created emotional experiences, attracting like-spirited people who created their own products to sell outside of the concert venues. Stadium parking lots were converted into marketplaces—and the followers of the band shared their stories and their lives with others in the community. The Grateful Dead culture is not created by Madison Avenue but by an endearing mission and trusting relationships.

EXPERIENCE. Founder Jerry Garcia had a transcendent mindset about the band and music. "For me, it's always emotional—can I live with the song? I'm going to have to get on stage and be this song. I'm going to have to represent this point of view, this idea. And if it doesn't work for me, I can't do it. I can't act, you know? So there has to be something authentic about it." Music and business today have become way too transactional, almost boring at times. Organizations must be willing to go to the edge to birth amazing experiences. The Dead didn't just embrace the *experience economy*; they embodied it.

Barry Barnes, author of *Everything I Know About Business I Learned from the Grateful Dead*, wrote, "The band was always open to 'start over.'" Do you operate with that level of freedom?

WHAT NOW?

When does your lack of authenticity show up? What does it cost you, and what one thing can you practice today to live more honestly?

"To be yourself in a world that is constantly trying to make you something else is the greatest accomplishment."

RALPH WALDO EMERSON

A PURPOSEFUL
GROWTH MINDSET

"Becoming is better than being."

CAROL DWECK

Growing up I was the athlete in our family, and my younger brother Don had other interests. He entirely changed his tune later in life, first falling in love with long-distance running and now competing in marathons and iron man competitions. This same mentality caused him to shift gears and become a therapist in the San Francisco area after years in the Chicago advertising industry. My little brother Don, along with his partner Pavel, has never been fearful of stepping into his identity. He lives his life open minded and open hearted. He embraces learning, is a positive influence on his clients, and loves to learn. My little brother is the embodiment of the growth mindset.

Over the last thirty years of assessing the mindset of top performers, I am convinced that the best in every industry possess a growth mindset. What separates the good from the great is the embracing of personal growth. Carol Dweck, professor of psychology at Stanford University, has "mainstreamed" the idea of cultivating a growth mindset while minimizing the risks associated with a fixed or a limited mindset.[173] People who willingly accept a growth mindset reconsider what personal failure and challenge means to them.

People with a fixed mindset believe their skills, talents, and intelligence are static or fixed. In other words, we are born with it. This leads to a life of not welcoming self-development. They also believe that skills, not effort, drive success. Leaders with a fixed mindset avoid challenges and may get defensive and discouraged very quickly. This is very limiting and hinders performance.

In a growth mindset, people believe effort—accompanied with talent—is the blueprint for growth. They are learners, and they are very tenacious. They believe challenges must be embraced and are an opportunity for growth. When hitting a challenge, they see it as an opportunity for a shift. Dweck's research has found that almost all high performers possess a growth mindset.

Which attributes distinguish the good from the elite?

- **SELF-DIRECTION.** My research shows this to be the single most powerful differentiator. Top performers don't need to be told what to do next; they enjoy risk taking, leading others, and assessing new opportunities. They are very coachable, are nondefensive, and encourage feedback.

- **RESILIENCE.** We all fail and suffer from occasional defeat. People with growth mindsets accept this, learn from it, and move on quickly. They don't play the victim, blame others, or let failure define them. They have reframed what "losing" means. The cliché is true: failing opens one up to the potential to learn.

Carol Dweck reminds us in her book *The New Psychology of Success*, "We like to think of our champions and idols as superheroes that were born different from us. We don't like to think of them as relatively ordinary people who made themselves extraordinary." The most talented understand that growth is a choice.

In a world of great uncertainty, where the rules are changing right before our eyes, your ultimate secret weapon for creating competitive advantage is buried at your core.

The most talented understand that growth is a choice.

Some of the best titans of industry have one overwhelming similarity: their businesses are birthed from their mission. Innovation, differentiation, and internal growth all come from this one source. Purpose drives growth, not the other way around.

Your distinct corporate identity and mission matter. And if it doesn't truly compel others, it may instead be repelling those you hope to inspire.

A recent *Fast Company* article titled "Generation Flux" brilliantly conveyed the value of flexibility and purpose by asking various leaders in business to discuss their missions. Bounce these ideas around your next team meeting.

- Apple CEO Tim Cook emphasizes purpose-driven social goals over financial goals as a symbol to lead his organization. "We do things because they're just and right."[174]

- Eileen Fisher, CEO and founder of the Eileen Fisher Fashion Company, goes even further: "We want to be a great company more than we want to be a big company. If selling more means creating more stress for ourselves, should we do it?"[175]

- Robert Wong, executive creative director of Google Creative Lab, said, "The manager era is gone. Your staff can leave. They have the option to go. That's why purpose is so important. It's the best way to keep talent."[176]

Everyone wants to work on a team that leaves an imprint and allows for growth. We all want to be inspired by what we do, believing it matters. Mission matters, and it could be your secret weapon for driving change.

WHAT NOW?

When does your fixed mindset show up? What does it cost you, and what one thing can you practice today to champion a relaxed, growth mindset with your team?

"Never look down to test the ground before taking your next step; only he who keeps his eye fixed on the far horizon will find his right road."

DAG HAMMARSKJOLD

REFLECTION TIME

QUESTIONS TO PONDER

1. How are you at discussing risks, threats, or challenges, and are you memorable or agreeable?

2. A thoughtful question is more powerful than a good answer. What question should you now ask?

3. Where do you need to focus, and what do you need to learn to become distinct?

4. Your best new customers are your existing customers. How are you protecting your core?

5. Do you collaborate and codesign custom solutions with customers, associates, and teammates?

6. Do you holistically understand your customers' agenda, discussing mutual purpose not products?

7. Is the soul of your team recognized without ever having to say a word?

8. Purpose is normally not discovered; it's uncovered. What's your team's purpose?

9. Have you ever considered choosing to be distinct instead of big? Compelling instead of perfect?

10. Do you blame, play victim, or let defeats define you, or do you reframe challenges as learning?

ACTION MATTERS

"If someone offers you an amazing opportunity but
you are not sure you can do it, say yes—then learn
how to do it later!"

RICHARD BRANSON

Blind spots trip us up, yet they are part of being human. This book is a synthesized summation of ten years of research, coaching, and rethinking different moments in my life. We are all a work in progress, and I hope you have taken good notes. There are ideas in this book worth discussing with your friends, family, and colleagues. Yes, personal change at times is very challenging, but that is also part of being human. Think through which of the ideas detailed in this book speaks to you loudest

The most interesting people I know are dedicated to their own self-development.

and commit to reread that chapter a few more times. The most interesting people I know are dedicated to their own self-development.

- **HOW DO YOU AFFECT OTHERS, AND WHAT MUST YOU LEARN, RELEARN, OR UNLEARN TO BE EFFECTIVE?**

- **WHAT BLIND SPOTS NEGATIVELY AFFECT YOUR RELATIONSHIPS AND PERSONAL PERFORMANCE?**

- **ARE YOU AS RELEVANT TO YOUR COMPANY, CUSTOMERS, AND FRIENDS AS YOU THINK?**

- **ARE YOU PRESENT AND EMBRACING THE MOMENT WITH OTHERS?**

- **ARE YOU EFFECTIVE AT SHARING YOUR STORY WITH PEOPLE UNLIKE YOURSELF?**

- **WHAT IS YOUR INNER SPARK, AND ARE YOU ON A COMPELLING MISSION?**

- **WHAT IS YOUR OPTIMAL PSYCHOLOGY AND MINDSET THAT ENHANCES YOUR LIFE?**

- **WHAT GETS IN THE WAY OF YOUR ABILITY TO EXECUTE YOUR OWN PERSONAL PLAN?**

Whether you're in a position of leadership or not, we all own how we show up and affect others. Too often, we fall into the same problematic traps. We lack courage in difficult times when a leap of faith is needed, and we deceive ourselves into believing changes are impossible. The most common and sneaky blind spot, however, is the tendency to take yourself out of the game before it even starts by playing too safe.

There are hundreds of ideas detailed within this book. Go back and think about how you can include some of these ideas within your team, family, or relationships. Is there one personal, relational, or organizational blind spot that you should commit to focus on?

Recently I spoke with an old friend who was frustrated over previous life decisions that took him far away from the things he truly valued: family, friends, and making a difference in others' lives. After twenty minutes of reminding me of every mistake he had ever made, I paused and reminded him of something he had forgotten. I shared, "There's still time to change your story." He then paused and said, "I would love to create a new story." If you feel you need to create a new story, know you are not alone.

"When you are transparent, vulnerable, and courageous, you are halfway there."

WHAT'S NEXT? WORKSHEET

PART I: PERSONAL

WHAT IS THE POTENTIAL BLIND SPOT?	WHAT BEHAVIOR WILL YOU PRACTICE?
When does your imposter show up? What does it cost you, and what one thing can you practice today to embrace your true self?	
When does your lack of self-awareness show up? What does it cost you, and what one thing can you practice today to expand your self-awareness?	
When does overconfidence show up? What does it cost you, and what one thing can you practice today to minimize your overconfidence?	
When do your insecurities show up? What do they cost you, and what one thing can you practice today to neutralize your insecurities?	

When does your lack of curiosity show up? What does it cost you, and what one thing can you practice today to embrace a more curious mindset?	
When do your limiting beliefs show up? What do they cost you, and what one thing can you practice today to unlearn or let go of old beliefs or behaviors that no longer serve you?	
When does your fear show up? What does it cost you, and what one thing can you practice today to embrace your fears?	
When does your lack of humility show up? What does it cost you, and what one thing can you practice today to embrace humility?	
When does your lack of openness show up? What does it cost you, and what one thing can you practice today to embrace more openness?	
When do triggers show up? What do they cost you, and what one thing can you practice today to see yourself more clearly?	

When does closing your mind show up? What does it cost you, and what one thing can you practice today to promote inquisitiveness?	
When does distraction show up? What does it cost you, and what one thing can you practice today to improve your focus?	
When does your stubbornness show up? What does it cost you, and what one thing can you practice today to reassess your status?	
When does your lack of under-standing show up? What does it cost you, and what one thing can you practice today to critique your professional competitive position?	
When does your anxiety show up? What does it cost you, and what one thing can you practice today to invite structure and solitude into your life?	
When does defensiveness show up? What does it cost you, and what one thing can you practice today to better share your personal or company story?	

When do uncertainty and fear show up? What do they cost you, and what one thing can you practice today to increase your feeling of safety?	
When does your lack of self-reflection show up? What does it cost you, and what one thing can you practice today to increase deep work?	
When do your bad habits show up? What do they cost you, and what one thing can you practice today to build on your rituals, routines, and structure?	

PART II: RELATIONAL

WHAT IS THE POTENTIAL BLIND SPOT?	WHAT BEHAVIOR WILL YOU PRACTICE?
When does pessimism show up? What does it cost you, and what one thing can you practice today to model thankfulness within your team?	
When does lack of trust show up? What does it cost you, and what one thing can you practice today to promote confidence and trust with others?	

When does self-centeredness show up? What does it cost you, and what one thing can you practice today to embody selflessness?	
When does your lack of transparency show up? What does it cost you, and what one thing can you practice today to strengthen your partnerships?	
When does your lack of empathy show up? What does it cost you, and what one thing can you practice today to convey understanding to others?	
When does fear of losing control show up? What does it cost you, and what one thing can you practice today to empower others?	
What drains your energy? What does it cost you, and what one thing can you practice today to prioritize life-giving activities?	
When does your impulsiveness show up? What does it cost you, and what one thing can you practice today to accentuate win-win discussions?	

When does your lack of courage show up? What does it cost you, and what one thing can you practice today to embody directness with others?	
When does lack of judgment show up? What does it cost you, and what one thing can you practice today to repair a broken relationship?	
When does your opposition to others' ideas show up? What does it cost you, and what one thing can you practice today to be inclusive?	
When do your wrongful assumptions show up? What do they cost you, and what one thing can you practice today to exhibit empathetic listening skills?	
When does your lack of questioning show up? What does it cost you, and what one thing can you practice today to invite others to question you?	
When does your excessive nature show up? What does it cost you, and what one thing can you practice today to truly simplify complexity in your life?	

When does your lack of preparation show up? What does it cost you, and what one thing can you practice today to be one with your audience?	
When does your lack of flexibility show up? What does it cost you, and what one thing can you practice today to epitomize the "Yes, and" mentality?	
When does your lack of clarity show up? What does it cost you, and what one thing can you practice today to express more conciseness?	
When does lack of alignment show up? What does it cost you, and what one thing can you practice today to understand others' unstated needs?	

PART III: ORGANIZATIONAL

WHAT IS THE POTENTIAL BLIND SPOT?	WHAT BEHAVIOR WILL YOU PRACTICE?
When do volatility, uncertainty, complexity, and ambiguity knock you off your game? What does it cost you, and what one thing can you practice today to dance with VUCA?	

When does your lack of purpose show up? What does it cost you, and what one thing can you practice today to solidify your personal purpose statement?	
When does your lack of cooperation show up? What does it cost you, and what one thing can you practice today to facilitate open discussions with others?	
When does your lack of planning show up? What does it cost you, and what one thing can you practice today to start creating a blueprint that clearly defines your goals?	
When does your lack of coaching courage show up? What does it cost you, and what one thing can you practice today to demonstrate fearless and thoughtful coaching?	
When does your lack of holistic thinking show up? What does it cost you, and what one thing can you practice today to engage others with your whole brain?	

When does your lack of internal motivation show up? What does it cost you, and what one thing can you practice today to build a healthy, internally inspired team?	
When do feelings of overwhelm show up? What do they cost you, and what one thing can you practice today to focus on the 20 percent of activities that matter most?	
When do you waste others' time with irrelevant information? What does it cost you, and what one thing can you practice today to design inspirational meetings?	
When does your failure to create emotional experiences with others show up? What does it cost you, and what one thing can you practice today to illustrate experiential leadership with others?	
When does your lack of risk aversion show up? What does it cost you, and what one thing can you practice today to epitomize more agility, flexibility, and comfort with change?	

When does your lack of collaboration show up? What does it cost you, and what one thing can you practice today to truly cocreate with your partners?	
When does your lack of team soul show up? What does it cost you, and what one thing can you practice today to bring SOUL to your team?	
When does your apathy show up? What does it cost you, and what one thing can you practice today to show positive intent and likeability to associates, customers, and your peers?	
When does your lack of grit show up? What does it cost you, and what one thing can you practice today to disrupt the status quo?	
When do your personal biases show up? What do they cost you, and what one thing can you practice today to be more coachable and teachable?	

When does your lack of authenticity show up? What does it cost you, and what one thing can you practice today to live more honestly?	
When does your fixed mindset show up? What does it cost you, and what one thing can you practice today to champion a relaxed, growth mindset with your team?	

DAN MACK

Managing Director,
Mack Elevation

Dan Mack is a strategist, advisor, and performance coach to numerous companies in the consumer package goods industry. He is the founder of the **Elevation Forum Leadership Group,** and he facilitates thought leadership events bringing together retailers and suppliers to discuss higher level partnerships and the future of the industry.

Mack researches and advises companies on the practices of holistic growth companies. His work was chronicled in his first book *Dark Horse: How Challenger Companies Rise to Prominence*. His second book, *Look Closer: Ideas on Reexamining and Eliminating Personal, Relational, and Organizational Blind Spots* is a blueprint to help leaders rethink how they personally and professionally engage the world.

Mack was a National Sales Training and Leadership Development Manager at GlaxoSmithKline, served as Vice President of Sales North America at GOJO Industries (the creator of PURELL), and Vice President of Sales North America at DenTek Oral Care. He's been published in Forbes on personal impact, performance coaching, and transformation.

Dan has a passion for coaching leaders on creating high performing cultures, personal influence, and team alignment.

ENDNOTES

1   Dr. Steve Maraboli, Life, the Truth, and Being Free (Better Today Publishing, 2009).

2   Brené Brown, The Gifts of Imperfection (Hazelden Publishing, 2010).

3   Dr. Travis Bradberry, TalentSmartEQ, https://www.talentsmarteq.com/articles/How-Successful-People-Overcome-Toxic-Bosses-779784437-p-1.html/.

4   "How the Imposter Syndrome is Holding You Back," Journal of Behavioral Science, https://www.nbcnews.com/better/health/how-impostor-syndrome-holding-you-back-work-ncna814231.

5   Brennan Manning, Abba's Child: The Cry of the Heart for Intimate Belonging (NavPress Publishing Group, 1994).

6   Manning, Abba's Child.

7   The Economist Executive Education Navigator, https://real-leaders.com/author/the-economist/.

8   Daniel Goleman, Emotional Intelligence (Bantam, 1995).

9   Dr. Steve Bressert, https://www.siliconrepublic.com/advice/personality-key-to-success.

10   Marshall Goldsmith, "Success Delusion," https://www.marshallgoldsmith.com/articles/success-delusion/.

11   Tasha Eurich, "What Self-Awareness Really Is (and How to Cultivate It)," Harvard Business Review, January 2018, https://hbr.org/2018/01/what-self-awareness-really-is-and-how-to-cultivate-it.

12   Jeff Miller, "More Than Half of New Managers Fail," Inc., September 2017, https://www.inc.com/jeff-miller/more-than-half-of-new-managers-fail-heres-how-to-a.html.

13   Patrick Lencioni, The Five Dysfunctions of a Team (Jossey-Bass, 2002).

14   Walter Isaacson, Steve Jobs (Simon & Schuster, 2011).

15   Walter Isaacson, interview by Adam Grant, 2018, http://knowledge.wharton.upenn.edu/article/leonardo-da-vinci-steve-jobs-benefits-misfit/.

16   Walter Isaacson, Leonardo da Vinci (Simon & Schuster, 2017).

17   Warren Berger, in conversation with Shane Parrish, 2016, https://fs.blog/2016/06/warren-berger-system-questioning/.

18   Thomas Kuhn, The Structure of Scientific Revolutions (University of Chicago Press, 1962).

19   Warren Buffet, Berkshire Hathaway Shareholder letter, 2017.

20   Charlie Munger, https://constantrenewal.com/avoiding-stupidity/.

21   Mark Bonchek, "Why the Problem with Learning is Unlearning," Harvard Business Review, https://hbr.org/2016/11/why-the-problem-with-learning-is-unlearning.

22   Atul Gawande, The Checklist Manifesto: How to Get Things Right (Picador Press, 2011).

23   John H. "Jack" Zenger and Joe Folkman, https://hbr.org/2015/11/we-like-leaders-who-underrate-themselves.

24   McKinsey study, https://www.imd.org/research-knowledge/articles/ why-you-will-probably-live-longer-than-most-big-companies/.

25   Tim Wilson quote, https://observer.com/2016/12/research-reveals-five-powerful-rituals-that-will-make-you-resilient/.

26   Jim Haudan, "How to Create an Environment That Fosters Truth Telling," Inc., December 2016, https://www.inc.com/jim-haudan/how-to-create-an-environment-that-fosters-truth-telling.html.

27   "The Beatles' Decca Audition," https://en.wikipedia.org/wiki/The_Beatles %27_Decca_audition.

28   Warner Bros., https://www.classicfilmfreak.com/2010/03/29/the-brothers-warner-2008-a-dvd-documentary-by-cass-warner-sperling/.

29   Marshall Goldsmith, Triggers (Crown Business, 2015).

30   Shunryu Suzuki, Zen Mind, Beginner's Mind (Weatherhill, 1970).

31   David Allen, Making It All Work (Penguin Publishing Group, 2009).

32   Christian Nellemann, "Don't Bore Your Customers," LinkedIn, April 2017, https://www.linkedin.com/pulse/dont-bore-your-customers-christian-nellemann, https://www.sciencedaily.com/releases/ 2008/04/080414145705.htm.

33   PwC Survey, https://www.pwc.com/gx/en/ceo-survey/2015/assets/ pwc-18th-annual-global-ceo-survey-jan-2015.pdf.

34   University of California–Davis study, http://blogs.ucdavis.edu/ egghead/2014/10/02/curiosity-helps-learning-and-memory/.

35   Suzuki, Zen Mind.

36   Mathew A. Killingsworth and Daniel T. Gilbert, "Wandering Mind Not a Happy Mind," Harvard Gazette, https://news.harvard.edu/gazette/story/2010/11/wandering-mind-not-a-happy-mind/.

37   Cheryl Conner, "Fifty Essential Mobile Marketing Facts," Forbes, November 2013, https://www.forbes.com/sites/cherylsnappconner/2013/11/12/fifty-essential-mobile-marketing-facts/#1ef6fd177475.

38   Peter Drucker quote, https://www.marshallgoldsmith.com/articles/teaching-leaders-what-to-stop/.

39   Rita Gunther McGrath, The End of Competitive Advantage: How to Keep Your Strategy Moving as Fast as Your Business (Harvard Business Review Press, 2013).

40   The Conference Board, https://www.conference-board.org/.

41   Fred Reicheld quote, Bain Consulting, https://www.bain.com/.

42   Sydney Finkelstein, Why Smart Executives Fail: And What You Can Learn from Their Mistakes (Portfolio, 2004).

43   Adam Grant, Originals (Viking, 2016).

44   Andy Grove, Only the Paranoid Survive (Profile Business, 1988).

45   McGrath, End of Competitive Advantage.

46   Adam Grant, "The Problem with Saying 'Don't Bring Me Problems, Bring Me Solutions,'" Harvard Business Review, September 2017, https://bit.ly/3jMFyCf.

47   Jackson G. Lu, Modupe Akinola, and Malia Mason, "To Be More Creative, Schedule Your Breaks," Harvard Business Review, https://hbr.org/2017/05/to-be-more-creative-schedule-your-breaks.

48   Susan Cain, Quiet: The Power of Introverts in a World That Can't Stop
      Talking (Crown Publishing Group, 2012).

49   David Allen, Getting Things Done (Penguin Publishing Group, 2001),
      and Making It All Work, (Penguin Publishing Group, 2009).

50   Howard Gardner, quoted in Richard L. Daft, The Leadership Experience
      (2014), 273.

51   Dan and Chip Heath, Made to Stick (Random House, 2007).

52   Peter Forbes quote, https://www.chelseagreen.com/writer/peter-forbes/.

53   Jimmy Neil Smith quote, https://www.ethos3.com/2017/12/21-amazing-
      quotes-about-storytelling/.

54   Paul Zak, "This is Your Brain on Storytelling: The Chemistry of Modern
      Communication," Forbes, https://www.forbes.com/sites/giovannirodri-
      guez/2017/07/21/this-is-your-brain-on-storytelling-the-chemistry-of-
      modern-communication/#2df0760ac865.

55   Harris Eisenberg, "Humans Process Visual Data Better," September 2014,
      http://www.t-sciences.com/news/humans-process-visual-data-better.

56   J. R. R. Tolkien, letter to his son Christopher (January 30, 1945), in
      The Letters of J.R.R. Tolkien (1981), 110.

57   Judith Glaser, Conversational Intelligence (Routledge, 2016).

58   Cal Newport, Hidden Brain podcast, https://www.npr.org/2017/07/
      25/539092670/you-2-0-the-value-of-deep-work-in-an-age-of-distrac-
      tion.

59   Jennifer Porter, "Why You Should Make Time for Self-Reflection
      (Even If You Hate Doing It)," Harvard Business Review, March 2017,
      https:// hbr.org/2017/03/why-you-should-make-time-for-self-reflection-
      even-if-you-hate-doing-it.

60   Tristan Harris, "How Technology Hijacks People's Minds," May 2016, http://www.tristanharris.com/essays/.

61   Giada Di Stefano. Gary P. Pisano, Francesca Gino, and Bradley Staats, The Role of Reflection in Individual Learning, Harvard Business School, 2014 https://www.hbs.edu/faculty/.../14-093_defe8327-eeb6-40c3-aafe-26194181cfd2.pdf.

62   "Penalty Kicks…By the Numbers," April 2009, The Science of Soccer, http://www.scienceofsocceronline.com/2009/04/penalty-kicks-by-numbers.html.

63   Marshall Goldsmith, Triggers (Crown Business, 2015).

64   Robert Hogan, https://www.hoganassessments.com/six-lessons-leadership-bob-hogan/.

65   Gallup, "Why Great Managers Are So Rare," https://www.gallup.com/workplace/231593/why-great-managers-rare.aspx.

66   Blake Thorne, "How Distractions at Work Take Up More Time Than You Think," 2015, http://blog.idonethis.com/distractions-at-work/.

67   Deloitte, https://www2.deloitte.com/us/en/pages/about-deloitte/articles/burnout-survey.html.

68   Jeffrey Pfeffer, Dying for a Paycheck: How Modern Management Harms Employee Health and Company Performance and What We Can Do about It (HarperCollins, 2018).

69   Shawn Achor, The Happiness Advantage (Crown Business, 2010).

70   Annie McKee, How to Be Happy at Work (Harvard Business Review Press, 2017).

71   PwC, Global CEO Survey, https://www.pwc.com/gx/en/ceo-survey/2017/pwc-ceo-survey-report-2017.pdf.

72   McCann research, https://adage.com/article/special-report-4as-confer-ence/mccann-survey-finds-half-america-trust-brand/308544.

73   Paul J. Zak, "The Neuroscience of Trust," Harvard Business Review, https://hbr.org/2017/01/the-neuroscience-of-trust.

74   Ashley Merryman, "Leaders Are More Powerful When They're Humble, New Research Shows," Washington Post, December 8, 2016, https://www.washingtonpost.com/news/inspired-life/wp/2016/12/08/leaders-are-more-powerful-when-theyre-humble-new-research-shows/?noredirect=on&utm_term=.d222c2a4ba4f.

75   Bradley Owens and David Hekman, "How Humble Leadership Really Works," Harvard Business Review, https://hbr.org/2018/04/how-humble-leadership-really-works.

76   Jack Welch, Winning (Harper Collins, 2005).

77   Heidi Grant Halvorson, No One Understands You and What to Do About It (Harvard Business Review Press, 2015).

78   Carol Dweck, Mindset: The New Psychology of Success (Random House, 2006).

79   Bain & Company survey, https://www.bain.com/insights/closing-the-delivery-gap-newsletter/.

80   Bain Report, Barriers and Pathways to Sustainable Growth: Harnessing the Power of the Founder's Mentality, https://www.bain.com/insights/founders-mentality-barriers-and-pathways-to-sustainable-growth/.

81   Marc Beaujean, Jonathan Davidson, and Stacey Madge, "The Moment of Truth in Customer Service," McKinsey Quarterly, February 2006, https://www.mckinsey.com/business-functions/organization/our-insights/the-moment-of-truth-in-customer-service.

82   Scott Galloway, "Innovative Leadership," talk, UC Berkeley Haas School of Business, April 2016, https://www.youtube.com/watch?v=QN9F WjxSOKU.

83   Brené Brown, "Empathy Is the Remedy," Psychology Today, https://www.psychologytoday.com/us/blog/partnering-in-mental-health/201408/bren-brown-empathy-vs-sympathy-0.

84   Roman Krznaric, Why It Matters, and How to Get It (TarcherPerigee, 2014).

85   Beth Mirza, "Toxic Workplace Cultures Hurt Workers and Company Profits," SHRM, September 25, 2019.

86   Randstad US, "Your Best Employees Are Leaving. But Is It Personal or Practical?," August 28, 2018.

87   Roselinde Torres, Peter Tolman, Susie Grehl, and Eva Sage-Gavin, "Good Vibrations: The CEO's Practical Guide to Create and Amplify Energy," Boston Consulting Group, May 2016, https://www.bcg.com/en-us/publications/2016/leadership-talent-people-organization-good-vibrations-ceos-practical-guide-create-amplify-energy.aspx.

88   Tony Schwartz, The Power of Full Engagement (Simon & Schuster, 2003).

89   The Cambridge Negotiations Lab, University of Cambridge, Judge Business School, Negotiation Training Program.

90   Fierce, Inc., Toxic Employees Survey 2017, August 2017.

91   Globis and PDC Consulting, The Difficult Conversations Survey, https://static1.squarespace.com/static/5a2eec3518b27d0e34328cf4/t-/5a60a63a24a694c1165d99e0/1516283462153/38-Reasons-The-Difficult-Conversations-Survey-2016.pdf.

92   Susan Scott, Fierce Conversations, Revised and Updated (New American Library, 2017).

93   Douglas E. Hughes, The Journal of Personal Selling & Sales Management (M.E. Sharpe, 1980).

94   Tomas Chamorro-Premuzic, "Why Others Might Not Trust You as Much as You Think They Should," Fast Company, June 2016, https://www.fastcompany.com/3061197/why-others-might-not-trust-you-as-much-as-you-think-they-should.

95   John Ellett, "B2B Buyers Don't Trust Vendors," Forbes, https://www.forbes.com/sites/johnellett/2018/10/10/b2b-buyers-dont-trust-vendors-and-that-is-a-huge-opportunity-for-marketers/#19ac03266a01.

96   Daniel C. Dennett, Intuition Pumps and Other Tools for Thinking (W.W. Norton Company, 2013).

97   Alex C. Huynh, "To Defuse an Argument, Think About the Future," https://hbr.org/2017/01/to-defuse-an-argument-think-about-the-future.

98   Rasmus Hougaard, Jacqueline Carter, and Gitte Dybkjaer, "Spending 10 Minutes a Day on Mindfulness Subtly Changes the Way You React to Everything," Harvard Business Journal (January 2017).

99   Henri Nouwen, quote, https://henrinouwen.org/meditation/where-to-put-our-attention/.

100   Isidor Isaac Rabi, quote, https://www.nytimes.com/1988/01/19/opinion/l-izzy-did-you-ask-a-good-question-today-712388.html.

101   Peter Abelard, quote, Readings in European History, Vol. I (1904), edited by James Harvey Robinson, 451.

102   Robert Altman quote, https://www.goodreads.com/quotes/search?utf8=%E2%9C%93&q=robert+altman&commit=Search.

103   Five Trends in Leveraging Leadership Development to Drive a Competitive Advantage, Bersin by Deloitte Research Bulletin, https://legacy.bersin.com/uploadedfiles/Five-Trends-ARC.pdf.

104   Dan and Chip Hearth, Made to Stick (Random House, 2007).

105   "The Moment of Truth in Customer Service," https://www.mckinsey.com/business-functions/organization/our-insights/the-moment-of-truth-in-customer-service.

106   Glenn Wilson, "The Lost Art of Concentration: Being Distracted in a Digital World," https://www.theguardian.com/lifeandstyle/2018/oct/14/the-lost-art-of-concentration-being-distracted-in-a-digital-world.

107   Adrian Ward, "The Neuroscience of Everybody's Favorite Topic," Scientific American, 2013, https://www.scientificamerican.com/article/the-neuroscience-of-everybody-favorite-topic-themselves/.

108   Bruce Springsteen quote, https://www.pbs.org/newshour/show/bruce-springsteen-tackles-truth-song-memoir.

109   "Humans Process Visual Data Better," September 2014, http://www.t-sciences.com/news/humans-process-visual-data-better.

110   Kelly Leonard and Tom Yorton, Yes, and (Harper Collins, 2015).

111   Three Seconds: The First Impression—Books to Courses, https://www.bookstocourses.com/tools/oc/.../Three_Seconds__The_First_Impression.

112   Daniel Kahneman, Thinking Fast and Slow (Farrar, Straus and Giroux, 2011).

113   Kevin McSpadden, "You Now Have a Shorter Attention Span Than a Goldfish," Time, May 2015, http://time.com/3858309/attention-spans-goldfish/.

114   Ward, "Neuroscience."

115   Mark Twain quote, https://www.brainyquote.com/quotes/mark_twain_
       100433.

116   John Holland, Customer Centric Selling, http://customercentric.com/
       blog/.

117   John Batiste quote, https://www.smithsonianmag.com/arts-culture/
       why-jon-batiste-perfect-choice-be-late-night-bandleader-180956296/.

118   The Tim Ferriss Show Transcripts: Jerry Seinfeld—A Comedy Legend's
       Systems, Routines, and Methods for Success (#485), December 2020.

119   Daniel Kahneman and Amos Tversky's Prospect Theory, https://www.
       nngroup.com/articles/prospect-theory/.

120   "Americans are More Anxious Today Than a Year Ago," https://
       www.usnews.com/news/health-care-news/articles/2018-05-08/
       study-americans-are-more-anxious-today-than-a-year-ago.

121   NN/g, Nielsen Norman Group, "Prospect Theory and Loss Aversion:
       How Users Make Decisions," https://www.nngroup.com/articles/
       prospect-theory/.

122   Bill Walsh quote, https://www.championshipcoachesnetwork.com/
       public/461.cfm.

123   Patrick M. Lencioni, "Make Your Values Mean Something," Harvard
       Business Review, https://hbr.org/2002/07/make-your-values-mean-
       something.

124   Yvon Chouinard, Let My People Go Surfing: The Education of a
       Reluctant Businessman (Penguin Books, 2005).

125   Lou Gerstner, Who Says Elephants Can't Dance? (Harper Collins, 2002).

126   Bloomberg stat, https://www.forbes.com/sites/ericwagner/2013/09/12/five-reasons-8-out-of-10-businesses-fail/#7cd883ff6978.

127   Peter Drucker, The 5 Most Important Questions You Will Ever Ask About Your Organization (Jossey-Bass, 2008), https://visionroom.com/sums/Sums-The-Five-Most-Important-Questions.pdf.

128   Peter Economy, "5 Essential Questions for Entrepreneurs," Inc., https://www.inc.com/peter-economy/5-essential-questions-entrepreneurs.html.

129   Peter Densen, "Challenges and Opportunities Facing Medical Education," Transactions of the American Clinical Association (2011), https://www.ncbi.nlm.nih.gov/pmc/articles/PMC3116346/.

130   GALLUP 2021 Workplace Study, "What Is Employee Engagement and How Do You Improve It?," https://www.gallup.com/workplace/285674/improve-employee-engagement-workplace.aspx.

131   Ned Herrmann, Whole Brain® Thinking, https://www.herrmannsolutions.com/what-is-whole-brain-thinking-2/.

132   John P. Kotter, What Leaders Really Do (Harvard Business School, 1990).

133   Rosabeth Moss Kanter, "Smart Leaders Focus on Execution First and Strategy Second," Harvard Business Review, https://hbr.org/2017/11/smart-leaders-focus-on-execution-first-and-strategy-second.

134   "Bill George: The Hierarchical Leader is Out. The Empowering Leader is In," Fortune, http://fortune.com/2015/08/03/bill-george-leadership-ceos/.

135   Gallup, State of the American Workplace, https://www.gallup.com/workplace/238085/state-american-workplace-report-2017.aspx.

136   "Impact of Team Performance Survey," http://www.thinkwiseinc.com/impact-of-team-performance-survey-report.html.

137   Sam Walker on John Eades podcast, https://www.linkedin.com/pulse/4-communication-hacks-great-leaders-dont-ignore-john-eades/?trk=eml-email_feed_ecosystem_digest_01-recommended_articles-9-Unknown&midToken=AQFfCb-wDPsW-g&fromEmail=fromEmail&ut=0pfOXCC0VjXoE1.

138   Alex Pentland, "The New Science of Building Great Teams," Harvard Business Review, https://hbr.org/2012/06/the-new-science-of-building-gr-2.

139   Scott Keller and Mary Meaney, Leading Organizations: 10 Timeless Truths (Bloomsbury Business, 2017).

140   Cal Newport, Deep Work (Grand Central Publishing, 2016).

141   George Ilian, 50 Life and Business Lessons from Steve Jobs (GeorgeIlian.com, 2015).

142   John Kenneth Galbraith, https://www.yorkpress.co.uk/news/3215988.meetings-are-indispensable-when-you-dont-want-to-do-anything/#:~:text=19th%20July%202007-,%E2%80%9CMeetings%20are%20indispensable%20when%20you%20don,t%20want%20to%20do%20anything%E2%80%9D&text=This%20is%20a%20quote%20from,%2C%20the%20Canadian%2DAmerican%20economist.

143   Perry Marshall, 80/20 Sales and Marketing (Entrepreneur Press, 2013).

144   Richard Koch, The 80/20 Principle: The Secret to Achieving More with Less (Crown Business, 1999).

145   Highfive blog, https://highfive.com/blog/10-video-conferencing-statistics.

146   Harvard Business Review, https://hbr.org/2017/07/stop-the-meeting-madness.

147   Roger Schwarz, Smart Leaders, Smarter Teams (Jossey-Bass, 2013).

148   Matthew Dixon and Brent Adamson, The Challenger Sale (Penguin Random House 2011).

149   McKinsey, "How to Create an Agile Organization," 2017, https://www.mckinsey.com/business-functions/organization/our-insights/how-to-create-an-agile-organization.

150   Klaus Schwab, The Fourth Industrial Revolution (World Economic Forum, 2016).

151   Why Business Agility Matters, https://www.pega.com/system/files/resources/2019-02/why-business-agility-matters.pdf.

152   Adam Robinson, "Want to Boost Your Bottom Line?," https://www.inc.com/adam-robinson/google-employees-dedicate-20-percent-of-their-time-to-side-projects-heres-how-it-works.html.

153   Jason Saltzman, "Why Agility is Key to Business Success," https://www.forbes.com/sites/forbesnycouncil/2018/04/03/why-agility-is-key-to-business-success/#6f837abd20f1.

154   Esteban Kolsky, "20 Stats to Customer Experience Enlightenment," September 2017, https://www.unicomcorp.com/blog/customer-experience-statistics-infographic/.

155   "Brands Co-Creating Their Futures with Millennials," YPulse, November 2014, https://www.ypulse.com/post/view/brands-co-creating-their-futures-with-millennials.

156   C. K. Prahalad and Venkat Ramaswamy, The Future of Competition: Co-Creating Unique Value with Customers (Harvard Business School Press, 2004).

157   Howard Schultz quote, https://hbr.org/2010/07/the-hbr-interview-we-had-to-own-the-mistakes.

158   Bo Burlingham, "The Coolest Small Company in America," Inc., 2003, https://www.inc.com/magazine/20030101/25036.html.

159   Bo Burlingham, Small Giants (Penguin Books, 2008).

160   Bruce Springsteen, Born to Run (Simon Schuster, 2016).

161   Steve Tobak, "The Surprising Truth About Likability," Entrepreneur, June 2017, https://www.entrepreneur.com/article/295392.

162   Black Swan blog, "3 Guidelines for Negotiating Like a Pro," http://blog.blackswanltd.com/the-edge/3-guidelines-for-negotiating-like-a-pro.

163   Lee Resources study, https://www.customerservicemanager.com/customer-service-facts/.

164   Jack Zenger and Joseph Folkman, "I'm the Boss! Why Should I Care if You Like Me?," Harvard Business Review, May 2013, https://hbr.org/2013/05/im-the-boss-why-should-i-care.

165   IRI, New Product Pacesetter, https://www.iriworldwide.com/en-US/insights/Publications/New-Product-Pacesetters-2016.

166   Jane Dunlevie, "As Emerging Brands Take Share, M&A Heats Up," https://www.goldmansachs.com/insights/pages/jane-dunlevie-m-and-a-heats-up.html.

167   CircleUp, Report: Small Brands Beat Big CPG's in Innovation, https://www.nosh.com/news/2017/report-small-brands-beat-big-cpgs-innovation.

168   Dan Mack, Dark Horse: How Challenger Companies Rise to Prominence (Sakura Publishing, 2013).

169   "Percentage of Global Research and Development Spending in 2018, by Industry," https://www.statista.com/statistics/270233/percentage-of-global-rundd-spending-by-industry/.

170   Ed Catmull, Creativity, Inc. (Random House, 2014).

171   Robert Cialdini, Influence: The Psychology of Persuasion (Harper Collins, 1984).

172   Barry Barnes, Everything I Know about Business I Learned from the Grateful Dead (Grand Central Publishing, 2011).

173   Carol Dweck, Mindset: The New Psychology of Success (Random House, 2006).

174   Tim Cook quote, "Generation Flux's Secret Weapon," Fast Company, October 2014, https://www.fastcompany.com/3035975/find-your-mission.

175   Eileen Fisher quote, "Generation Flux's Secret Weapon," Fast Company, October 2014, https://www.fastcompany.com/3035975/find-your-mission.

176   Robert Wong quote, "Generation Flux's Secret Weapon," Fast Company, October 2014, https://www.fastcompany.com/3035975/find-your-mission.

Made in United States
North Haven, CT
01 October 2022

24833734R00191